GENIUS
INTELLIGENCE:

Secret Techniques and Technologies to Increase IQ

THE UNDERGROUND KNOWLEDGE SERIES

**James & Lance
MORCAN**

GENIUS INTELLIGENCE: Secret Techniques and Technologies to Increase IQ

Published by:
Sterling Gate Books
78 Pacific View Rd,
Papamoa 3118,
Bay of Plenty,
New Zealand
sterlinggatebooks@gmail.com

Although the authors and publisher have made every effort to ensure that the information in this book was correct at press time, the authors and publisher do not assume and hereby disclaim any liability to any party for any loss, damage, or disruption caused by errors or omissions, whether such errors or omissions result from negligence, accident, or any other cause.

Should you the reader identify any content within this book that is harmful, hurtful, sensitive or insensitive, the authors and publisher ask that you contact them so they may rectify any problem.

Special Note: This title is an extended version of Chapter 5 of *The Orphan Conspiracies* (Sterling Gate Books, 2014) by James Morcan & Lance Morcan. This title therefore contains a combination of new material as well as recycled material (in many cases verbatim excerpts) from *The Orphan Conspiracies*.

National Library of New Zealand publication data:

Morcan, James 1978-
Morcan, Lance 1948-
Title: GENIUS INTELLIGENCE: Secret Techniques and Technologies to Increase IQ
Edition: First ed.
Format: Paperback
Publisher: Sterling Gate Books
ISBN: 978-0-473-31849-9

CONTENTS

CONTENTS

FOREWORD

This book is part of *The Underground Knowledge Series*, written by James & Lance Morcan, authors of a much needed, perceptive summary of the darker aspects of world reality titled *The Orphan Conspiracies*, which I also wrote a foreword for.

I was employed for many years as a senior research scientist developing naval underwater weapon systems at the Technical Research and Development Institute of the Ministry of Defense, Japan. During this period, I spent a lot of time in my private life studying *Number Theory*, which is a branch of pure mathematics devoted primarily to the study of the integers, or whole numbers.

From this mathematical research, I came across the enigma of Srinivasa Ramanujan (Figure 1), an Indian genius mathematician who, with almost no formal training, discovered many complex formulas and made extraordinary contributions to mathematical analysis and number theory. Ramanujan often said the Goddess of Namakkal inspired him with formulae at night while he was dreaming and that each morning, upon awakening, he would write down the results of these vivid dreams.

For many years, I could not understand the mental processes that lead to Ramanujan's advanced mathematical findings. However, after studying the human brain from the standpoint of superluminal particles, I eventually came to the conclusion that everyone's brain has the potential to connect to an outer field of consciousness, which has also been termed by more mystical thinkers as the Universal Mind.

To summarize my research on the brain, I wrote *Superluminal Particles and Hypercomputation*, which was published by LAMBERT Academic Publishing in early 2014. Soon after its publication, I was contacted by James Morcan, one of the authors of *Genius Intelligence*, who felt that my theories on superluminal particles could support his and Lance Morcan's suppositions about the nature of genius.

Figure 1: *Srinivasa Ramanujan*

This book you are now reading contains a wide range of genius methods – all of which have the potential to increase your IQ. You'll read about everything from speed reading to brain gland activation to sleep learning to smart drugs to virtual reality training.

I believe this is a much needed book for those who sense there are faster and easier ways to learn and study than the methods currently being taught in mainstream education systems.

Lastly, I sincerely hope that the publication of *Genius Intelligence* contributes to a global awakening to assist us to hold enough truth in our minds to change this world for better.

Dr. Takaaki Musha

Director of the Advanced-Science Technology Research Organization, Yokohama, Japan.

Former senior research scientist at the Technical Research and Development Institute of the Ministry of Defense, Japan.

INTRODUCTION

The genesis for this book was fiction rather than reality.

Now we've revealed that, you would be forgiven for assuming none of what follows on the mightily complex subject of intelligence and increasing IQ is true.

Before we attempt to put your mind at ease on that score, we have a few more revelations to get out of the way...

Neither of us has any formal education qualifications of note, having barely completed high school. Nor has either of us ever taken an IQ test and therefore it cannot be proven we have high intelligence just as it cannot be disproven we are complete idiots!

About now, you'd also be forgiven for asking why we, of all people, have written a book on intelligence and the nature of genius.

On the fiction versus reality issue, it's not quite as alarming as it sounds, we hope.

You see, the fictional reference actually relates to our international thriller series of novels titled *The Orphan Trilogy*.

The decision to write this thriller series was made a decade ago, and it marks the commencement of our journey. A journey to discover what makes a genius and, more importantly, what makes a genius tick.

In *The Ninth Orphan*, book one in the trilogy, our mysterious lead character (who is known only as Nine) is not only an assassin, but also a mental genius who exhibits a level of intelligence rarely if ever seen in any character in literature. Nine has a photographic memory, can read entire books in five minutes flat and speaks dozens of languages. Plus he learns new skills extremely fast and is highly adaptable – so much so he's nicknamed *the human chameleon*.

How Nine reached that level of intelligence, though, is merely implied or hinted at in the first book in the series.

In its prequel, *The Orphan Factory*, we had to design an education system that would reveal exactly how Nine and his fellow orphans grew up to become that smart. This was quite a challenge as our setting was no Ivy League college. Rather, it was the Pedemont Orphanage, a rundown institution in Riverdale, one of Chicago's poorest neighborhoods.

Having both gone through the traditional education system and finding it laborious and uninspiring, we quickly discovered it was fun to brainstorm alternative and more advanced forms of study for our trilogy. Even so, it took many years of investigating accelerated learning methods – some rare, some not so rare – before we felt confident enough to write about what it would take to create youngsters with intellects as advanced as those of our Pedemont orphans.

All the insights unearthed during that 10-year investigative period (spent examining the great historical minds and studying little-known intelligence boosting methods) are revealed in *Genius Intelligence*.

Highlights of our exploration into the world of super learning include many fascinating discoveries, which were totally new – to us at least and, we expect, in most cases will be new to you, too – and which were certainly outside our personal experience collectively and individually.

Those discoveries include:

- Individuals (living and dead) with IQ's far higher than Einstein's.

- Brain waves common to geniuses – and the various ways to induce those brain waves.

- Mental techniques the world's elite and A-List celebrities are quietly using to help them process information while they're asleep or in *virtual* worlds.

- Chemical substances students and academics the world over employ to kick-start the brain into overdrive.

- Cutting-edge technologies business tycoons and professional athletes employ to achieve a mental edge on their competitors.

Beyond these random examples, one of the key discoveries we made is that every human brain has enormous potential – possibly even *unlimited* potential.

No matter the challenging circumstances – whether ADHD, dyslexia or mental illness – it makes no difference when it comes to the brain's *latent* potential. The capacity for achieving genius levels of intelligence remains the same. After all, there has been many a genius with learning disabilities, hyperactivity and genetic brain disorders.

The latest scientific studies have revealed extraordinary findings. The brain is much more flexible and adaptable than previously thought. It can evolve and creatively work around limitations and nullify them.

Examples of this phenomenon even include brain-damaged individuals who have been shown to be capable of achieving equal intelligence to the average person.

How or why this is possible is because of the brain's incredible capacity to restructure itself.

This rewiring process falls under a category in neuroscience known as *neuroplasticity* – a broad term used to describe the brain's ability to form new neural connections or to reorganize itself in an attempt to overcome or diminish the effects of old age, substance abuse or traumatic head injury.

Neuroplasticity is scientific proof that intelligence is *not* something that is locked by a certain age or that cannot fluctuate or increase.

Not receiving a college degree or even a high school education doesn't mean genius abilities are out of the question. The same applies for those who come from a background of extreme poverty.

History is littered with examples of uneducated and semi-educated individuals from impoverished backgrounds who have gone on to educate themselves and deliver revolutionary breakthroughs within academic circles, the corporate world, the arts and other walks of life.

When the brain's potential is fully unleashed, there can be few if any limitations (Figure 2). Anyone who tells you otherwise isn't up-to-date with the latest scientific findings on the brain and is exhibiting their ignorance. For the brain's potential *is* the human potential...

The other crucial discovery – perhaps *the* most crucial – to come out of our research is that higher intelligence is not necessarily something you're born with or genetically predisposed toward. In fact, most instances of above-the-ordinary intelligences are usually *acquired* thru superior learning techniques – many of which we cover in detail in this book.

Reading about the greatest minds in history, including recent history, more often than not reveals the individuals concerned (or people close to them) employed specific learning methods. The examples we cite throughout this book shatter the myth that geniuses are always born with exceptional intelligence and/or talent.

Certainly, there are those born with amazing abilities not fostered by educational methods, but our research has revealed these naturally gifted geniuses are definitely the exception, not the norm.

A classic example of this natural born genius myth is Wolfgang Amadeus Mozart (Figure 3) whom most believe was simply a wunderkind, or virtuoso, from infancy. Many brain researchers have also described the Austrian composer as someone who just had incredible musical and artistic abilities from birth.

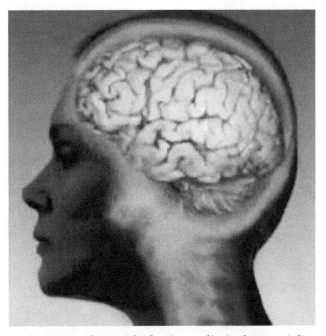

Figure 2: *Above: The brain...unlimited potential?*

"Human brain female side view"
by National Institute of Health

Licensed under Public Domain via Wikimedia Commons

Figure 3: Mozart as a child

"Wolfgang-amadeus-mozart 2" by Anonymous possibly by Pietro Antonio Lorenzoni (1721-1782) Portrait owned by the Mozarteum, Salzburg. Licensed under Public Domain via Wikimedia Commons

However, as with most geniuses, there is a significant body of evidence to support the contentious theory that Mozart's brilliance was as much the result of *nurture* as it was *nature*, if not more so.

It is true the musical prodigy was composing by five, and by seven or so he was performing for audiences throughout Europe. And while achievements like that, at those early ages, are certainly extraordinary, the key point is that Mozart came from a musical family and was pushed to excel musically. As soon as he could walk and talk, in fact, or even earlier if you stop to consider he was exposed to classical compositions while still in his mother's womb.

The young Mozart's father Leopold was a renowned composer in his own right and an ambitious musical teacher who wanted his son to achieve greatness. History tells us that Leopold forced Mozart Junior to practice for many hours a day even before he had reached school age.

It has been estimated that by the time Mozart was six he had already spent about 4000 hours studying music.

Perhaps a modern-day equivalent to Mozart's father would be someone like Richard Williams, father of legendary American tennis champions Serena and Venus Williams. Upon deciding tennis was the way out of the 'ghetto', Williams Sr. pushed his daughters day after day from a young age in his relentless quest for them to become world champions.

Classical music experts have noted that many of Mozart's childhood compositions are mostly rearrangements of other (older) composers' works. Not being experts in classical music – or any music for that matter – we can't comment, but if true that would further undermine the enduring myth about the great composer being an innate genius who could rely solely on his natural talent and who hardly needed to practice.

We found that nine out of ten biographies of geniuses reveal forgotten or previously unmentioned examples of intelligence-enhancing techniques and/or technologies these individuals employed on their path to greatness.

Traditionally, IQ has been perceived as a genetic trait in much the same way an individual's height or body type is perceived – in other words a fixed trait, or state, and therefore (thought to be) something that could never be altered.

In recent years, however, there has been an explosion of new scientific studies, which make a mockery of that assumption. These show that cognitive training, whether by mental techniques or brain enhancement technologies, can definitely deliver intelligence-boosting effects.

Certainly, you need some natural aptitude to excel in most facets of life – be it mental, physical or artistic – but if genius was simply a matter of inheriting good genes, then many more of us would be geniuses.

Anyway, we predict, or sincerely hope, that formal education will one day be reflective of what occurs within the fictional Pedemont Orphanage of our thriller series – minus the assassination training of course!

Equally, we firmly believe some if not most of the alternative learning methods mentioned in *Genius Intelligence* will eventually become the norm for students the world over.

To return to that other awkward subject – who we are and what the hell we are doing writing about the secrets of the genius mindset. Well, that's a trickier one to satisfy readers on so early in the piece...

All we can really say is we write fiction and non-fiction books and produce movies in our dual careers as authors and filmmakers. In our earlier careers, we have between us held a variety of positions in different fields spanning the arts, media, PR and retail sectors. Those positions include journalist, bookseller, publicist and newspaper editor.

So we shall have to leave it up to you as to whether you think this book is a work of "genius" or not.

One reason we wrote this book is because, in our opinion, most other titles on the subject of increasing intelligence make for disappointing reading. In the main, they are not written for the average person. They're written *for* academics *by* people with PhD's.

The end result, more often than not, are books that resemble academic text and which rarely venture beyond scientifically proven and well-established mainstream methodologies.

Paradoxical though it may sound, we are convinced that *not* being from the world of academia, or even being particularly studious, eminently qualified us to write this book. After all, we wrote it to empower the average individual – the 'common' working class person. We can relate to such people as that's exactly our background.

One thing we can promise is that after researching far and wide in some unusual and unlikely places, the pages of this book contain the most advanced accelerated learning methods available on the planet.

Wishing you well on your path to increasing your IQ!

James Morcan & Lance Morcan

1

GENIUS TECHNIQUES OF THE ELITE

It has long been speculated that secret societies, mystery schools, intelligence agencies and other clandestine organizations have advanced learning methods superior to anything taught in even the most prestigious universities. Methods which are only ever taught to the chosen few – initiates who have all sworn an oath to keep the group's syllabus *in house* and never reveal any of the teachings to outsiders.

On the rare occasions the public get wind of these types of advanced learning techniques – usually via information leaked to the Internet, sometimes via published books – they are seldom tested or given the attention they deserve and so largely remain in obscurity. One reason for this could be the advanced techniques are often not comprehensible because whoever is behind them has withheld the overall curriculum.

There's many a tale of mysterious figures from secretive groups mastering skills, languages and even complex career paths so quickly that most would say it's impossible.

But that opinion assumes we common people know of, or have access to, all the learning methods known to man.

If we are to assume there are superior learning methods not taught in our mainstream education system then this naturally leads to other questions.

What if your child's top-notch education is actually a second-rate education?

Or, if you are a student, what if that professor you look up to is no mastermind, but just a tool of an inferior learning institution?

None of this is to disrespect formal education. It plays a vital role in society and the betterment of Mankind, and only a fool would doubt the importance of getting a good education.

Nor are we suggesting there isn't the odd learning institution that teaches at least some accelerated learning techniques, although such establishments would probably exist on the fringes of mainstream education.

Figure 4: *Roger Federer . . . Montessori alumni*

"R Federer Australian Open 2014"
by Peter Myers from Melbourne, Australia

Federer - Oz Open 2014. Licensed under CC BY 2.0 via
Wikimedia Commons

The Montessori system is possibly one such example as it allows children to have greater freedom of expression and to learn in playful and organic ways.

Successful alumni of the Montessori education system include Amazon founder Jeff Bezos, Nobel Prize-winning author Gabriel García Márquez, Wikipedia founder Jimmy Wales, tennis champion Roger Federer (Figure 4) and Google co-founders Sergey Brin and Larry Page.

In general, however, accelerated learning methods are more likely to be found outside the modern education system.

Let's face it, wherever in the world you go, real prodigies are the exception not the norm in the present system. Those rare individuals whom society labels as geniuses are almost always *freaks of nature* and are *naturally gifted* rather than being diligent students who became geniuses as a result of their education.

"I'll be a genius and the world will admire me. Perhaps I'll be despised and misunderstood, but I'll be a genius, a great genius."

~ *Salvador Dalí.*
Written in his diary at the age of 16.

2

POLYMATHS AND HIGH-IQ INDIVIDUALS

"The purpose of having the orphans study all these diverse fields was not for them to just become geniuses, but to become polymaths – meaning they would be geniuses in a wide variety of fields. Whether they were studying the sciences, languages, international finance, politics, the arts or martial arts, they would not stop until they'd achieved complete mastery of that subject. Kentbridge himself had encyclopedic knowledge about almost everything, and expected nothing less from his orphans."

~ *The Ninth Orphan*

A book critic who reviewed *The Ninth Orphan*, book one in our thriller series, criticized our protagonist Nine (the ninth-born orphan) for having an IQ, or intelligence quotient, higher than Einstein's. The strong implication in the review was that this was a ridiculous character decision we, the authors, had made.

That all sounds like a valid criticism on the surface, but had this critic gone beyond his own sphere of knowledge and done a little research he would have discovered there are many people whose IQ's have been recorded to be higher than Einstein's.

American author Marilyn Vos Savant, for example, has an IQ of 192; Russian chess grandmaster and former world champion Garry Kasparov has an IQ of 194. Incidentally, Einstein's IQ was estimated in the 1920's to between 160 and 190.

But wait, there's much more when it comes to the world of super geniuses . . .

Quite a few individuals have tested in excess of a 200 IQ score, including South Korean civil engineer Kim Ung-yong (210), former child prodigy and NASA employee Christopher Hirata (225) and Australian mathematician Terence Tao (225-230).

And last but not least is American child prodigy, mathematician and politician William James Sidis who had an IQ of 250-300 (Figure 5). He graduated grammar school at age six, he

Figure 5: *Sidis . . . 20th Century child prodigy*
"William James Sidis 1914" by Unknown - The Sidis Archives.
Licensed under Public Domain via Wikimedia Commons

went to Harvard University at age 11 and graduated *cum laude* at the age of 16. Sidis, who died in 1944, could fluently speak 40 languages by the time he reached adulthood.

Remember, the average IQ is 100 and approximately 50% of those tested score between 90 and 110.

According to the book *IQ and the Wealth of Nations*, by Dr. Richard Lynn and Dr. Tatu Vanhanen, the top five countries in terms of average IQ's of their citizens are Hong Kong (107), South Korea (106), Japan (105), Taiwan (104) and Singapore (103). Further down the list, China, New Zealand and the UK share equal 12th position with a 100 average, while the US is in 19th position with an average citizen IQ of 98.

However, many scholars in the 21st Century now believe IQ scores aren't everything and it's likely areas of intelligence exist that cannot be measured in any test. This is possibly substantiated by the number of successful and iconic individuals who recorded very low IQ scores. These include the once highly articulate and outspoken boxer Muhammad Ali who, as a young man, scored only 78 – an IQ so low it supposedly denotes a mild mental disability!

And of course, the list of the world's so-called most intelligent *excludes* extremely bright individuals in impoverished parts of the world where IQ's are, or were, rarely tested. The Indian mathematical genius, Srinivasa Ramanujan (1887-1920), was an example of such incredible geniuses who defy all explanation.

You'll recall Dr. Takaaki Musha refers to Ramanujan in the Foreword, mentioning how he was inspired by the gentleman's advanced mathematical findings.

Born into poverty in Erode, India, Ramanujan discovered extraordinary mathematical formulas despite being self-taught with no formal training in mathematics. He changed the face of mathematics as we know it and left many highly-educated and acclaimed Western mathematicians completely gobsmacked.

Furthermore, the other high-IQ individuals mentioned earlier are only in the top bracket of those who *agreed* to undergo IQ tests *and* allow their scores to be published.

It's quite conceivable certain elite individuals belonging to secret societies, mystery schools or intelligence agencies do not reveal their IQ scores. That secret intelligence factor was the basis for our fictional Pedemont orphans in *The Orphan Trilogy* whom we either state or imply have IQ's of around 200 or higher.

As a result of the accelerated learning techniques within the diverse curriculum that begins before they can even walk or talk, the orphans can assimilate and retain phenomenal amounts of information. By their teens, the child prodigies are more knowledgeable even than adult geniuses. They can solve complex problems, are fully knowledgeable about almost any current world subject or historical event, and are to all intents and purposes organic supercomputers and human library databases.

Our orphans are exposed to highly advanced learning methods so that they will have at their disposal all the necessary skills and information to be able to overcome life-and-death problems that may arise on future espionage assignments. They're taught there is no challenge or question that cannot be overcome, solved or answered as long as they fully utilize the power of their minds.

Each child at the Pedemont Orphanage eventually becomes a *polymath* – a person who is beyond a genius. It's a word we use throughout the trilogy as we felt it best describes the orphans' off-the-scale intellects.

A polymath is actually a *multiple-subject genius*. However, the criterion for a polymath is someone who is an expert in vastly different, almost unrelated fields. For example, an artist who works in the film, theatre and literary industries and who is a masterful actor, screenwriter, novelist, film director and film producer would *not* qualify as a polymath as those fields are all artistic mediums and closely related.

Rather, a polymath is someone who has excelled in, or completely mastered, a variety of unrelated or loosely related subjects. These

Figure 6: *Portrait of Leonardo da Vinci c. 1510*

*"Francesco Melzi - Portrait of Leonardo - WGA14795" by
Francesco Melzi*

*Web Gallery of Art. Licensed under Public Domain via
Wikimedia Commons*

Figure 7: *Leonardo da Vinci's The Vitruvian Man*

"Da Vinci Vitruve Luc Viatour" by Leonardo da Vinci

Own work www.lucnix.be. 2007-09-08 (photograph).

Photograph: This image is the work of Luc Viatour / www.Lucnix.be

could be as diverse as economics, dance, architecture, mathematics, history, forensic science, cooking and entomology.

And before you go calling yourself a polymath, don't forget you must be an *expert* i

each field. Unfortunately being a jack-of-all-trades and master-of-none doesn't count.

One of the best examples of a polymath is Leonardo da Vinci (Figure 6).

Born in Italy in 1452, Leonardo was a sculptor, painter, architect, mathematician, musician, engineer, inventor, anatomist, botanist, geologist, cartographer and writer. Although he received an informal education that included geometry, Latin and mathematics, he was essentially an *autodidact*, or a self-taught individual.

The man who many have called *the* most diversely talented person who ever lived, left behind an array of masterpieces in the painting world alone, including *The Last Supper*, *Mona Lisa* and *The Vitruvian Man (Figure 7)*.

"The knowledge of all things is possible"

~ Leonardo da Vinci

3

OUTRUNNING THE CONSCIOUS MIND

"The subconscious was always favored over the everyday conscious mind, which was considered too slow to be effective."

~ *The Orphan Factory*

Developing a genius mindset essentially comes down to two things: operating at speed and using the subconscious mind more than the conscious. This intuitive or relaxed approach to study is the polar opposite of traditional and mainstream forms of education.

Apart from some artistic subjects like music or dance, learning institutions generally require pupils to concentrate hard at all times. In other words, students have no choice but to always use their conscious minds, thereby suppressing the great reservoir of the subconscious.

When we are forced to think s-l-o-w-l-y like this our brain functions at well below optimum levels. That's why school students often feel exhausted as studying in this fashion is incredibly draining.

But how can we feel mentally drained when neuroscientists and brain researchers agree we each only use a tiny percentage of our brain?

In *The Orphan Trilogy*, our orphans often go into a daydream state whenever they need answers to life-and-death situations. This is because when you defocus you allow your intuitive self, or your subconscious mind, to *deliver* the answers you need. It just happens, without reaching for it.

We've all experienced pondering a problem all day long only to find we *receive* the solution when forgetting about the problem and thinking of something else. When we stop concentrating so hard, we allow our subconscious to flourish, and those who do this more than others are sometimes called geniuses.

As head of the Pedemont Orphanage, Tommy Kentbridge says to his students in *The Orphan Factory*, "The subconscious mind is where all higher intelligences exist. Every genius throughout history – Tesla, Einstein, Da Vinci – tapped into the infinite power of their subconscious minds."

Studies have shown the subconscious mind can process around 11 million bits of information per second. The conscious mind, however, can only process about 15 to 16 bits of information per second.

Quite a difference!

One of the best ways to bring the subconscious mind into the equation is to *outrun* the conscious mind by going so fast it literally can't keep up. So, at Chicago's Pedemont Orphanage, our orphans do everything at speed. They're also taught how to learn things indirectly instead of directly. By skirting around the edges of complex subjects, the children never get information overload or lose their way.

As we wrote in *The Ninth Orphan*, "In the tradition of Leonardo da Vinci and history's other great polymaths, the children were taught how to fully understand anything by using an advanced mental technique where they would simply *life* their minds into comprehension."

To life your mind into comprehension is once again the polar opposite of modern education systems which imply there's only one way to learn: consciously and with intense concentration.

While this indirect way of learning may sound flaky, it is actually backed up by hard science and is not remotely mystical. This approach is about brainwaves and understanding, or recognizing, the optimal state for learning.

When you hit the right groove, it's possible to learn quickly and in a satisfying, even enjoyable, fashion.

It is that singularity of mind top sportsmen and martial arts masters achieve. Psychologists sometimes refer to this ultimate mental state as *the zone*, but it's really just about having the most effective brainwaves for learning.

Any time study feels laborious the student is most likely in the beta brainwave, which occurs when the conscious mind is governing. A beta-dominant mind is the perfect recipe for mediocrity and boredom.

The subconscious mind comes into play in other less common brainwaves such as alpha, gamma, theta and delta. These brainwaves have also been shown to be activated when test subjects are laughing, daydreaming, meditating, singing, dancing or spontaneously moving about.

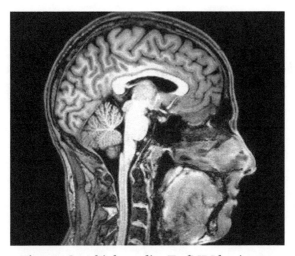

Figure 8: *A high quality T3 fMRI brain scan*
"FMRI Brain Scan" by DrOONeil - Own work.
Licensed under CC BY-SA 3.0 via Wikimedia Commons

Now how many math or English teachers would tolerate those activities in their classrooms?

What if there really is a much quicker, less methodical way of learning that allows you to learn without learning?

Sounds paradoxical, doesn't it?

"Talent hits a target no one else can hit. Genius hits a target no one else can see."

~ *Arthur Schopenhauer*

4

SPEED-READING

"The early development of speed reading can be traced to the beginning of the (20th) century, when the publication explosion swamped readers with more than they could possibly handle at normal reading rates."

~ Tony Buzan

One of the most important skills our Pedemont orphans possess is the ability to speed read. Having vast amounts of knowledge, or being *walking encyclopedias*, is a common trait in geniuses, and even more so in polymaths.

Probably the simplest way to gain this amount of knowledge is to learn to read very, very fast.

Speed-reading is therefore at the core of the radical education program we designed in our conspiracy thriller series.

However, our orphans' technique is much more advanced than the majority of speed-reading programs currently available to the public. Many such programs simply offer complementary reading skills rather than allowing for a whole new way to absorb the written word.

As we say in *The Ninth Orphan*, "It wasn't so much speed-reading as mind photography – a technique where the practitioner taps into the brain's innate photographic memory. The orphans were taught how to use their eyes and open their peripheral vision to mentally photograph the page of a book, magazine or newspaper at the rate of a page per second. Then they'd consciously recall every detail as if they'd read the material at normal, everyday reading speed. Tens of thousands of books, on all manner of subjects, were sent to the Pedemont Orphanage to keep up with the children's prolific reading habits."

The technique we wrote about was inspired by the most sophisticated speed-reading methods in the real world, as well as analysis of renowned speed-readers. It's also based on the brain's scientifically proven ability to pick up things subliminally and rapidly. By incorporating peripheral vision and photographic memory, it's possible to mentally scan or *photograph* entire pages at a time rather than one word at a time.

This method enables the Pedemont orphans to read at the rate of about 20,000 words per minute. That's many times faster than most readers can manage. In fact, the average reading speed is only 300 words per minute, or about one page per minute.

Although some skeptics – along with one or two book critics who reviewed our thriller series – have expressed doubt over whether the human brain can absorb such vast quantities of data all at once, speed-reading is not fiction. And it has some famous devotees.

Various US Presidents were confirmed or rumored speed-readers. They include Theodore Roosevelt, Franklin Roosevelt, John F. Kennedy (Figure 9) and Jimmy Carter.

Theodore (Teddy) Roosevelt, a self-taught speed-reader, is reported to have read a book before breakfast every single day while serving as president. Teddy's recall was said to be perfect and he would often quote from the books he read.

Kennedy studied under American speed-reading expert Evelyn Wood who could read at an impressive 6000 words a minute. JFK claimed he could read at around 2000 words per minute with a very high comprehension rate.

Carter, who also studied speed-reading during his time in the White House, took courses with his wife Rosalynn and their daughter Amy (Figure 10).

The fact that Dwight D. Eisenhower said "Don't be afraid to go in your library and read every book" may well allude to the fact he was yet another US president who could speed read. After all, who else but a speed-reader would have the time or ability to read *every* book in their local library?

Bestselling author, life coach and motivational speaker Anthony Robbins practices speed-reading and recommends it to audiences, personal clients and his readers.

In 2007, when J.K. Rowling's *Harry Potter and the Deathly Hallows* was published, six-time world champion speed-reader Anne Jones was the first to read it. Jones finished the 200,000-word, 759-page hardcover book in 47 minutes flat. Immediately afterwards, she completed a book review and sent it out to media outlets to prove her total comprehension of the story.

Jacques Bergier, French Resistance fighter, spy, journalist, chemical engineer and author of the bestselling book *The Morning of the Magicians*, was a born speed-reader. He started reading magazines and newspapers as a toddler, and by the age of four was fluent in three languages. By the time he reached adulthood, Bergier was reading 10 books a day.

Figure 9: *JFK . . . speed reading President*
"John F. Kennedy, White House photo portrait, looking up"
by White House Press Office (WHPO)
Licensed under Public Domain via Wikimedia Commons

Figure 10: *President Carter speed reading with his daughter Amy.*

Amy Carter and Jimmy Carter participate in a speed reading course at the White House.

NARA - 173797" by Unknown or not provided

U.S. National Archives and Records Administration.

Licensed under Public Domain via Wikimedia Commons

New Yorker and State University graduate Howard Berg was listed in the 1990 Guinness Book of World Records as the world's fastest reader. His reading speed was clocked at a remarkable 25,000 words per minute. Berg says his skill was developed out of boredom. He spent his childhood in the library, which was apparently the only place in the world that interested him.

Autistic savant Kim Peek (1951- 2009) (Figure 11) was one of the world's foremost speed-readers. The real-life inspiration for Dustin Hoffman's character in the 1988 movie *Rain Man*, Peek read at between 10,000 and 20,000 words per minute and had a 98% comprehension rate. His method was to read two pages simultaneously, one with each eye. Spending most of his days in the public library in Salt Lake City, Utah, Peek read many thousands of books.

Of all the examples of speed-readers, living or deceased, Peek's methods are closest to those described in *The Orphan Trilogy*. We sincerely hope in years to come scientists will figure out exactly how Peek so readily absorbed information from books so that children can be taught the technique the world over.

Figure 11: *Kim Peek . . . the real Rain Man*
"Kim Peek, diagnosed with Savant syndrome"
Licensed under Attribution via Wikimedia Commons

"In junior high, Robbins took a speed-reading course and began consuming what would be nearly 700 books through high school, mostly on psychology and personal development."

~ December 27, 2013 article about Anthony Robbins in Investor's Business Daily.

Since the term *speed-reading* was coined by Evelyn Wood more than 50 years ago, the skill has featured in various TV series and Hollywood movies.

In the 1996 feature film *Phenomenon*, lead character George Malley, played by John Travolta, exhibits extraordinary speed-reading skills.

Dr. Spencer Reid, one of the main characters on the hit TV series *Criminal Minds*, is also a speed-reader.

There's a speed-reading scene in the 2004 spy film *The Bourne Supremacy*, starring Matt Damon, in which CIA agent Pamela Landy, played by Joan Allen, is seen reading agency files at rapid speeds. Landy uses her finger to run up and down over text on each page. This finger pointing method is a real speed-reading technique known as Meta Guiding.

In *Good Will Hunting* – another Matt Damon movie – Damon, who plays natural-born genius Will Hunting, is seen alone in his apartment flipping through page after page of a book without pause.

Whether these two films on the actor's resume are just a coincidence or whether he's a closet speed-reader himself is anyone's guess.

"Modern research has shown that your eye-brain system is thousands of times more complex and powerful than had previously been estimated, and that with proper training you can quickly reap the benefits of this enormous potential."

~ *Tony Buzan*

In summary, any seeker serious in becoming a genius should put speed-reading at or near the very top of his or her list of necessary skills to acquire.

We recommend avoiding any of the common speed-reading courses that mention terms and phrases like *chunking*, *skimming*, *skim-reading* or *reading whole sentences at a time* – or indeed any courses that only promise students the ability to read two to five times quicker than the average reader.

Instead, we advise seeking out less common reading methods that claim to allow readers to absorb knowledge at or close to one page per second reading speeds. At least 10,000 words per minute would be a wise guideline for pursuing the most advanced reading systems. Signs of super advanced speed-reading techniques are the use of such terms as *peripheral vision, reading photographically, subliminal learning, limbic system, subconscious reading, photographic memory* and *the midbrain* in any promotional material.

5

BRAINWAVE ENTRAINMENT

"With the help of virtual reality and biofeedback technologies, the orphans were taught how to guide their minds to reach certain brain frequencies – like Alpha, Theta and Delta – at will. The purpose of slipping into these particular frequencies was to allow the right brain to take over, as opposed to the left-brained consciousness dominant in most people. Whenever the orphans needed to access their higher intelligences, they would enter a daydream and simply intuit the answers. That way, they could bypass thinking, and just know. Within the

Omega family, intuition was favored over logical thought patterns."

~ *The Ninth Orphan*

As mentioned, brainwaves are a crucial part of accelerated learning techniques. It's proven that when individuals move out of normal waking brainwaves (beta) into other brainwaves (alpha, theta, delta and gamma) they enter the ideal state in which to absorb new information. Whether the learning is analyzing complex equations, or memorizing facts, or becoming an expert in martial arts, it makes no difference.

Our children at the Pedemont Orphanage use brainwave generators and biofeedback machines to reach the optimal frequency for study. This method of altering the mind is known as *brainwave entrainment*.

Gamma brainwaves, which are the highest frequency brainwave, are held in high regard at the orphanage.

As we wrote in *The Orphan Factory*: "The children performed mind photography in uncommon brainwaves for regular wakeful consciousness. In this case it was predominantly gamma waves, and it allowed them to tap into the genius of their subconscious minds."

Besides being present while learning languages or forming new ideas, Gamma waves are also vital for recalling memories. And the faster the gamma brainwave, the faster the

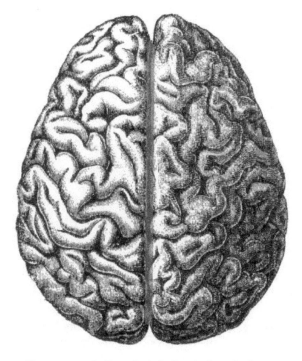

Figure 12: *Left and right brain hemispheres*
"Human brain longitudinal fissure" by Gray
Licensed under Public Domain via Wikimedia Commons

Figure 13: *Dr. Patrick Flanagan with the latest model of his Neurophone invention.*

memory recall is – yet another advantage in doing things at speed.

A common goal in most brainwave entrainment technologies or techniques is *hemispheric synchronization*. This ideal state occurs when the right and left hemispheres of the brain become harmonized or *in synch* and share similar or identical brainwaves. Studies have shown that when individuals have both hemispheres operating in similar brainwaves like this they are far more likely to learn and digest new information.

Furthermore, from such studies it is also apparent that most high IQ individuals, and those whom society describes as geniuses, have their brain hemispheres in synch more often than the average person.

In some cases this is a form of conscious self-programming where the genius is fully aware of the ideal brain state he or she needs to be in to perform complex mental feats – and also has the ability to mentally guide him or herself at will into hemispheric synchronization.

In many other cases, however, it is just a fortunate skill they have been born with, and the individual is completely unaware of their good luck in inheriting such a tool. Geniuses who lived before the invention of EEG equipment and the discovery of specific types of brainwaves would likely fit into this category.

Some modern brainwave technologies used to achieve hemispheric synchronization include biofeedback machines, purposefully designed audio recordings (such as binaural beats, monaural beats and isochronic tones), and hypnagogic light and sound machines.

Another impressive technology that has been shown to significantly alter brainwaves and put users in the ideal state for learning is Dr. Patrick Flanagan's *Neurophone* (Figure 13).

Invented in 1958 when Flanagan was only 13 years old, the Neurophone is a US-patented electronic nervous system excitation device that transmits sound to the brain through the skin and via the nervous system.

The invention earned the American doctor a profile in a 1962 edition *Life* magazine while he was still in his teens. *Life* referred to him as a "unique, mature and inquisitive scientist." His website mentions Dr. Flanagan "has continued to develop the Neurophone and it is currently being sold as an aid to speed learning."

6

SLEEP-LEARNING

*"While the child was asleep, a
broadcast programme from London
suddenly started to come through; and
the next morning . . . Little Reuben woke
up repeating word for word a long
lecture by that curious old writer . . .
The principle of sleep-teaching, or
hypnopædia, had been discovered . . .
The principle had been discovered; but
many, many years were to elapse
before that principle was usefully
applied . . . They thought that
hypnopædia could be made an
instrument of intellectual education."*

~ Aldous Huxley, Brave New World.

Even at night, the Pedemont orphans' education continues through hypnopædia, or sleep-learning. Audio courses play through headphones they wear and our orphans are able to learn new subjects like high finance or foreign languages while asleep.

Hypnopædia comes from the Greek *hypnos*, meaning 'sleep,' and *paideia*, meaning 'education.'

Although still not conclusive, some research has shown the subconscious mind is very receptive to absorbing knowledge whilst we sleep.

There are numerous references to hypnopædia in Aldous Huxley's 1932 dystopian novel *Brave New World*.

Thirty years later, this unusual learning method was also mentioned in *A Clockwork Orange*, another dystopian novel, by Anthony Burgess.

The popularity of these bestselling novels coincided with the release of positive results of preliminary studies into sleep-learning, ensuring that hypnopædia became relatively well known around the world and interest in it blossomed.

However, from the early 1960's onwards, more in-depth scientific studies were conducted in laboratories in the US and the UK, disproving the theory that humans could learn during sleep.

Figure 14: *Aldous Huxley . . . hypnopædia believer*
"Aldous Huxley" by Not given - Transferred from tr.wikipedia
Licensed under Public Domain via Wikimedia Commons

Even though many students in numerous countries kept claiming they achieved better exam results after listening to audio recordings on subjects whilst asleep, official studies simply did not confirm this. As a result, hypnopædia was discredited for about 50 years and slipped into obscurity in scientific and education circles.

Only in the last few years has the potential learning method resurfaced. Recent studies are beginning to contradict earlier experiments and it may not be long before hypnopædia is proven to be a valid form of education.

For example, on August 29, 2012, *The Huffington Post* ran a news article under the headline *Sleep Learning May Be Possible: Study*. The article mentioned a new study by researchers at the Weizmann Institute of Science, which demonstrated test subjects learnt new information while asleep.

In an interrelated experiment, scientists at Illinois' Northwestern University discovered that taking a 90-minute nap immediately after studying helps solidify knowledge in the brain. They taught new things – both physical and mental – to people and then tested them on how well they remembered and applied the knowledge taught.

There were two groups involved: one whose members slept after learning and one whose members stayed awake the whole time. Those who slept in the lab after studying showed significantly better mastery of the subject matter when tested.

NBC's *Today* published an article about the subject on September 11, 2014 which concurred with other recent findings.

"Research is beginning to show that our brains don't go completely offline during a doze," the article states, "but are actually busy organizing and storing away memories of events — and may be quite open to other activities.

"In fact," the article continues, "a new study has shown that the brain can be started on a task just as a person is dropping off to sleep and then, during slumber, take in new auditory information and then process it, according to a report published Thursday in Current Biology."

So hypnopædia is once again on the scientific radar, and it may not be long before this unorthodox and rare technique is conclusively proven to be a genuine learning method. Until then, many students, professionals and academics will continue to listen to audio recordings as they sleep and many will also continue to provide positive testimonials.

7

BRAIN GLAND ACTIVATION

"As soon as they could walk and talk, he gave them activities designed to open up as many neural pathways in their brains as possible."

~ *The Ninth Orphan*

Activating dormant brain glands is another technique used inside the Pedemont Orphanage.

Studies have shown that all individuals have a certain amount of dormant or underdeveloped brain areas. Every human brain ever mapped scientifically has shown at least some inactive cells and neurons.

This area of neuroscience, especially concerning little known brain glands, may hold the answer as to why we only use such a small percentage of our brains.

Important and often dormant, semi-dormant or underutilized brain glands include fairly well known ones like the pineal gland (Figure 15). This powerful gland, which has been known about since ancient times, is said to be well developed in most persons of high intellect and produces the serotonin-derived hormone melatonin.

Less reported glands and interrelated areas of the brain include the pituitary (nicknamed the body's master gland) (Figure 15), which controls most other hormone-secreting glands, the thalamus (necessary for planning and decision-making), the amygdala, which can bypass thought and instantly react, the hippocampus (one of the only areas of the brain where *neurogenesis* or the birthing of new neurons can occur) and the hypothalamus (crucial for memory and learning).

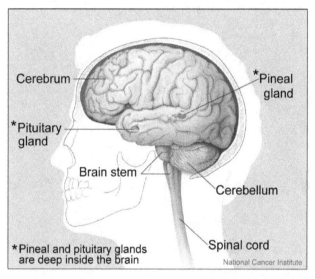

Figure 15: *The Pineal and Pituitary brain glands*

"Major parts of the brain" by Alan Hoofring (Illustrator)

National Cancer Institute, an agency part of the National Institutes of Health

Licensed under Public Domain via Wikimedia Commons

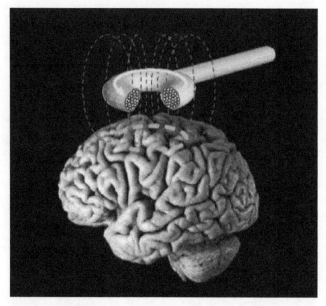

Figure 16: *TMS technologies stimulate the brain non-invasively*

"Transcranial magnetic stimulation" by Eric Wassermann, M.D. - Wassermann, Eric.

Transcranial Brain Stimulation. Behavioral Neurology Unit.

National Institute of Neurological Disorders and Stroke, National Institutes of Health,

United States Department of Health and Human Services.

Licensed under Public Domain via Wikimedia Commons

In *The Orphan Trilogy* we show how all these parts of the brain can be stimulated into activity in a variety of ways, including magnetism.

As we wrote in *The Orphan Factory*: "Rare earth magnets were embedded inside each helmet for the purpose of activating certain brain glands. Glands that were dormant in the average person."

Neuromagnetic helmets and similar brain stimulation technologies are not just confined to the realms of fiction.

Transcranial direct current stimulation, or TDCS, is one type of brain stimulation technique used in the real world. It's carried out by applying a helmet or cap to the individual's head. TDCS targets specific parts of the brain with low voltage electrical currents. This allows for the alteration of electrical states of neurons in targeted areas of the brain.

TDCS is in its infancy, but early studies have shown it enhances motor skills, memory recall and concentration. As a result, the US military now employs TDCS to assist fighter pilots, snipers and other personnel.

In a BBC news article dated July 22, 2014, TDCS is explored in relation to making sleep-learning possible. "In the near future, technology may offer further ways of upgrading the brain's sleep cycles. Memory consolidation is thought to occur during specific, slow, oscillations of electrical activity, so the idea here is to subtly encourage those brain waves without waking the subject.

"Jan Born, at the University of Tubingen," the article continues, "has been at the forefront of these experiments. In 2004, he found that he could help amplify those signals using transcranial direct current stimulation (tDCS), which passes a small electric current across the skull, successfully improving his subjects' performance on a verbal memory test."

In 2013, several TDCS inventions became commercially available to the public for the first time.

Leading UK newspaper *The Guardian* ran an article on February 5, 2014 under the heading *Can an electronic headset make you a better video gamer?* The article mentions a specific device that "uses the principles of tDCS – transcranial direct current stimulation – sending a small current of between 0.8 and 2.0mA through the prefrontal cortex through electrodes positioned on your forehead."

Although the technology is still being refined, many video gamers all over the world are reporting increased mental concentration and better performance. This bodes well for other types of mental exercises – like academic study for example – especially as the TDCS devices become more honed.

Transcranial magnetic stimulation, or TMS (Figure 16), is a similar non-invasive brain enhancement technology except it uses magnets instead of electricity. TMS's magnetic fields are capable of altering neurons in targeted areas of the brain.

Neuromagnetic helmets and similar devices have been nicknamed 'zap caps' and preliminary studies show they have the potential to improve brain function in numerous ways.

Another article that ran in *The Guardian* nicely summarized a recent scientific study that proves TMS's positive influences on the brain. The August 2014 article states that "memory can be boosted by using a magnetic field to stimulate part of the brain, a study has shown. The effect lasts at least 24 hours after the stimulation is given, improving the ability of volunteers to remember words linked to photos of faces."

The Guardian article quotes Dr Joel Voss, from Northwestern University, in Chicago, as saying: "We show for the first time that you can specifically change memory functions of the brain in adults without surgery or drugs, which have not proven effective. This non-invasive stimulation improves the ability to learn new things."

The latest studies also show that TMS can specifically stimulate the hippocampus, which oversees and directs the entire brain including crucial glands. Formerly it was believed the hippocampus was too deeply embedded in the brain to be stimulated by TMS. However, scientists have recently discovered the hippocampus can be stimulated indirectly via connected brain structures within the reach of TMS's magnetic fields.

Another potential method of increasing activity in specific brain glands like the pituitary is by ingesting an unusual substance called Ormus. (See Chapter 11 for more on Ormus).

8

POLYGLOTS AND SAVANTS

The Pedemont orphans all speak a large number of languages and are therefore *polyglots*. Although we never actually specify how many, it's implied in our trilogy that each orphan can speak dozens of languages.

They also have the ability to learn new ones quickly, and more than once we show our orphans, or orphan-operatives, completely mastering languages in the days leading up to a new mission.

While this may seem far-fetched, there have been persistent reports of CIA agents mastering languages within one week. If true, this is most likely a direct result of *classified* learning techniques or brain technologies not available to the general public.

Besides speculation on secret language techniques and suppressed technologies in the world of espionage, is speed learning languages really possible?

In 2004, British autistic savant Daniel Tammet (Figure 17) shocked Icelandic peoples when he appeared on live television to demonstrate his almost-overnight mastery of their notoriously complex language. Tammet spoke fluent Icelandic, having only studied the language for seven days.

Besides savants like Tammet and others born with rare genetic gifts that allow for such rapid memorization skills, is polyglotism, or the ability to master multiple languages, achievable for the average person?

Yes.

Notable polyglots throughout history include the following (with numbers in brackets corresponding to the amount of languages they spoke fluently): Cleopatra (9), Mithridates VI of Pontus (22), John Milton (11), Noah Webster (23), Arthur Rimbaud (10+), Giuseppe Caspar Mezzofanti (39), Friedrich Engels (20+), Nikola Tesla (8), José Rizal (22), Harold Williams (58), Mahapandit Rahul Sankrityayan (36) and Kenneth L. Hale (50).

Memory is obviously a major part of mastering languages quickly. Perhaps one Joshua Foer, a former journalist who became a

Figure 17: *Linguistic savant Daniel Tammet*
"Daniel Tammet" by jurvets - Born on a Blue Day.
Licensed under CC BY 2.0 via Wikimedia Commons

Figure 18: Dr. Georgi Lozanov – creator of Suggestopedia.

"Lozanov 2008 at Viktorsberg" by Kazhagiwara - Own work.

Licensed under CC BY-SA 3.0 via Wikimedia Commons

mnemonist – someone with the ability to recall unusually long lists of data – has some answers for those desiring to be polyglots.

Foer authored the bestselling book *Moonwalking With Einstein: The Art and Science of Remembering Everything*, which chronicles his journey to becoming a memory expert. The book also describes how after only one year of training he was able to become USA Memory Champion.

"Memory is like a spiderweb that catches new information," Foer writes in *Moonwalking with Einstein*. "The more it catches, the bigger it grows. And the bigger it grows, the more it catches."

Irishman Benny Lewis is a contemporary polyglot who speaks 12 languages fluently. Lewis, who taught himself Dutch in only six weeks and proved it by recording a video of himself being interviewed in Dutch, runs a website devoted to teaching others how to speed-learn languages.

The self-confessed "mediocre student" has also published a book titled *Fluent in 3 Months: How Anyone at Any Age Can Learn to Speak Any Language from Anywhere in the World*, which has received excellent reviews.

"The book is everything I've learned in 11 years of full-time language learning," Lewis told UK news site *Metro* in an article dated March 13, 2014. "It's all the changes in mentality and, of course, the techniques, because there are plenty of tricks to mastering a language from scratch.

"Language books are generally written by people with PhDs in linguistics or born into multilingual environments and I didn't see anything that was relatable. I did poorly in school – barely passed German – and felt people would relate to that."

Some of Lewis' simple language learning techniques include: speaking the language from day one rather than studying text books; listening for specific words or segments you recognize rather than entire sentences; making vivid mental associations in order to remember certain words.

Bulgarian educator and psychiatrist Dr. Georgi Lozanov (1926-2012) (Figure 18) created an education system known as *Suggestopedia*, which is primarily used for speed learning languages.

Although Baroque and classical music is extensively used in the curriculum, Suggestopedia (also sometimes called Suggestopædia) involves a lot more than just listening to specific compositions. Essentially, the controversial and unproven learning method incorporates a combination of passive and active learning. It also employs various arts – including singing, music, drama and paintings – to put the mind in the most *suggestive* state for learning.

Admittedly, Dr. Lazanov's education system is not a conclusive method for speed learning foreign languages and has been written off as mere pseudoscience by some researchers. However, a report on Suggestopedia by the United Nations Educational, Scientific and Cultural Organization (UNESCO) makes for interesting reading.

Compiled by UNESCO education experts at a meeting in Sofia, Bulgaria in 1978, the report concludes: "There is consensus that Suggestopedia is a generally superior teaching method for many subjects and for many types of students, compared with traditional methods. We have arrived at this consensus following a study of the research literature, listening to the testimony of international experts, observing films portraying Suggestopedia instruction and visiting classes in which Suggestopedia is practiced."

Dr. Lazanov claimed throughout his career that foreign languages could be mastered in a tenth of the usual time by following his methods.

From the numerous examples listed in this chapter, it should be clear that learning multiple languages in rapid time is possible. And, unlike naturally-gifted savants such as Daniel Tammet, it should also be noted that Benny Lewis and many other historical and modern polyglots are essentially savants-by-training.

Therefore, it does indeed appear possible for the layman to acquire the necessary skills to become a polyglot.

9

VIRTUAL REALITY

"The world of reality has its limits; the world of imagination is boundless."

~ Jean-Jacques Rousseau (1712-1778)

Virtual Reality (VR) is another advanced learning technology utilized within the walls of the Pedemont Orphanage. However, we specify it's not VR as most of us know it.

This excerpt from *The Orphan Factory* explains what we are getting at: "Like most Omega technologies, it was a technology that was decades ahead of official science, and although virtual reality was widely known and available to the public, this military version had been suppressed from the masses because of its incredible power."

Although a suppressed form of the technology lies very much in government cover-up theories, known VR systems have already been proven to be effective in a wide variety of diverse fields.

Learning via this technology's computer-simulated environment is currently used the world over in the military, medical, aviation and architectural sectors to name but a few.

VR allows users to practice as if they are actually engaging in activities in the real world. The difference between reality and virtual reality can sometimes be so small it's indistinguishable to the human brain.

Or to put it another way, as we state in *The Orphan Factory*: "Carrying out assignments under the influence of this particular software was no different to performing them in real life – at least not as far as the mind was concerned."

An article on VR appeared in Forbes on October 31, 2014, with the bold heading *How Virtual Reality Could Transform Society*. The article mentions that besides the current application of the technology in video games, "the true value of VR may lay in other applications. The technology has serious implications for training, education and entertainment outside the traditional game space."

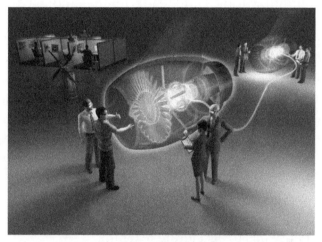

Figure 19: *A Virtual Reality learning environment.*

"ICIDO" by ICIDO GMBH - ICIDO GmbH.

Licensed under CC-BY-SA-3.0-de via Wikimedia Commons

The Forbes article goes on to say that one VR company "demonstrates VR's world-changing potential," adding that this manufacturer's version of the technology "could easily be used to transform military operational exercises, all kinds of training from medical to manufacturing and a host of other areas including social interaction, music, entertainment, communication, film, storytelling and having experiences that might otherwise not be possible such as free-falling, mountain climbing or swimming underwater for those incapable of doing it in reality."

One thing's for sure, the potential for students to learn with VR is staggering. This is exactly why various prestigious learning institutions, not to mention private individuals seeking to boost their IQ, are investing in VR headsets.

Here are just a few of the possibilities Virtual Reality has to accelerate learning:

- Studying with other students from all over the world in *virtual environments* that, for education purposes, will be no different to meeting face to face.

- Stimulating imagination and creativity in bigger and bolder ways like building bridges or cruise ships or directing explosive action sequences in blockbuster movies on virtual film sets.

- Doing things that are impossible in the real world such as transcending space and time by entering a VR simulated mock-up of ancient Egypt from a classroom.

VR will likely lead to endless possibilities throughout the 21st Century, and early adopters of this incredible technology may very well become more intelligent than those who are slower to embrace it.

10

SUPERLUMINAL PARTICLES

The physics of faster-than-light (also known as *superluminal*) phenomena may also hold great potential for accelerated learning.

Professor Regis Dutheil, a quantum physicist and consciousness researcher, was one of the first scientists to present a model that described the mind as a field of superluminal matter. He claimed that the human brain is an organic computer that transmits information.

According to Dutheil's theories, the mind, or consciousness, is essentially a field of tachyons or superluminal matter located on the other side of the light barrier in superluminal space-time.

In his book *L'homme Superlumineux*, Dutheil presents his hypothesis that consciousness is a field of superluminal matter belonging to the true fundamental universe and that our world is merely a subliminal holographic projection of it.

If you think Dutheil's theories sound a bit like the quantum physics concepts explored in the blockbuster Hollywood film *The Matrix*, you're not alone.

In his 2014 book *Superluminal Particles and Hypercomputation*, leading Japanese scientist Dr. Takaaki Musha (Figure 20) claims that the superiority of the human brain is due to the superluminal particles generated in the microtubules of the brain.

The blurb for *Superluminal Particles and Hypercomputation* mentions that the book "describes a series of theoretical explorations probing the possibility that superluminal particles exist, and if so the consequences their existence may hold for biology and computing. Starting from the standpoint of a model of the brain based on superluminal tunneling photons, the authors included in this volume have described theoretically the possibility of a brain-like computer that would be more powerful than Turing machines (conventional silicon processors), would allow non-Turing computations (hyper-computation), and that may hold the key to the origin of human consciousness itself."

A former senior employee of Japan's Ministry of Defense, where he developed naval weapon systems, Dr. Musha claims this generated superluminal field connects individuals with the outer field of the Universe, and he contends this may explain human consciousness as well as the collective mind of Mankind.

Dr. Musha's theory relates to the quantum mechanics scale known as *decoherence*, which measures the time to maintain the quantum coherence between particles. If the decoherence time is long in an individual's brain, it permits the person to connect to the outer superluminal field easily.

"I think that the activity of superluminal particles can be maintained by the structure of the metamaterial in the microtubules," says Dr. Musha. "The metamaterial has a non-natural property such as negative refractive index, which permits superluminal evanescent photons to move loosely in the nervous system. If this structure malfunctions in an individual, many problems can occur such as Alzheimer's disease."

Dr. Musha believes decoherence time can be extended by mental training. If this is true, then genius abilities like photographic memory and polymathing could result from the right sort of training.

If an individual's brain can connect with the superluminal field which is part of all other living organisms, then it may be possible for that individual to come from an awareness of what has been termed the *universal brain*.

Dr. Musha claims this could explain the extraordinary abilities of the human mind, such as the enigma of Indian mathematical genius Srinivasa Ramanujan.

Ramanujan found many mysterious formulas related to Number Theory and often said, "An equation for me has no meaning, unless it represents a thought of God."

Superluminal Particles and Hypercomputation also proposes that the true nature of the human electromagnetic field may be similar to that of the Universe as a whole.

Dr. Musha continues, "The ancient Indian Vedas texts have lent a comparable view of unified consciousness with a key difference being the process of human ascension from stage to stage. Instead of oneness with the Universe, the Vedic vision of consciousness emphasizes the importance of attaining knowledge and pure intelligence.

"This is similar to the Vedic concept that the totality of our consciousness is comprised of three levels: the subconscious, the conscious, and the superconscious mind. These levels of consciousness represent differing degrees of intensity of awareness. Intuition and heightened mental clarity flow from superconscious awareness. The conscious mind is limited by its analytical nature, and therefore sees all things as separate and distinct.

Figure 20: *Dr. Takaaki Musha*

Figure 21: *The famous red eye of HAL 9000*

"Logoparanobe" by Original uploader was Min's at fr.wikipedia

Transferred from fr.wikipedia; transferred to Commons by Commonlingua

Licensed under CC BY-SA 3.0 via Wikimedia Commons

"We may be puzzled by a certain situation because it seems unrelated to other events and it's difficult to draw a clear course of action. By contrast, because the superconscious mind is intuitive and sees all things as part of a whole, it can readily draw solutions.

"According to theoretical studies," Dr. Musha continues, "superluminal particles permit us to conduct infinite computations within a finite duration of time. Thus they can give us an extraordinary capability of computation, which is far greater than that of silicon processors."

Dr. Musha also believes if science can utilize superluminal particles for computer technology, it will one day be possible to build a hypercomputer system which has its own consciousness – like the HAL 9000 computer (Figure 21) in the Stanley Kubrick film, *2001: A Space Odyssey*.

The 2014 Luc Besson-directed film *Lucy* may also portray the superluminal field which is said to be omnipresent in the Universe. At the end of the film, Scarlett Johansson in the title role of genius Lucy becomes just that: *omnipresent in the Universe*.

Some of these superluminal theories about human intelligence may relate to what ancient mystics referred to as the Akashic field, which was said to be an etheric database of total knowledge about the Earth's entire history. If it is indeed possible to activate superluminal particles in the brain – whether by advanced yogic breathing techniques, smart drugs, or magnetic/electrical technologies to stimulate neurons – then perhaps every human really does have the potential to access this vast, invisible information field and prove that "the knowledge of all things is possible," as Leonardo da Vinci once stated.

However, for the time being at least, more research needs to be done on this particular field of science before geniuses can be created at will.

11

ORMUS

"The implications for creating a few geniuses or treating brain dysfunctions (using Ormus) are immense."

~ Lt. Lawrence F. Frego,
An End To All Disease

A mysterious substance known as *Ormus* – aka *ORME, White Powder Gold* or simply *White Gold* – is said by some to be another secret method used to increase intelligence.

In our novel *The Orphan Factory*, we show Ormus being given to the orphans every day at the Pedemont Orphanage. By ingesting it, the children activate their entire DNA/RNA cellular system, which not only unlocks their physical body's true potential, but also stimulates their conscious and subconscious minds.

We refer to how daily consumption of Ormus assists the orphans in every facet of their lives, from enhancing mental alertness to developing physical strength and endurance to promoting good health.

Although we include extensive references to it in that book and the rest of our *fictional* series, Ormus is actually a real substance discovered by science several decades ago.

As it has been said to balance both hemispheres of the brain and therefore allow for *whole brain learning*, it's being consumed the world over by people who are looking for safe and legal ways to increase their IQ. And the numbers using it are increasing every day as more and more people hear about it.

However, increasing IQ is said to be just the tip of the iceberg when it comes to this unusual scientific discovery which, we admit, sounds like something out of an episode of *The X-Files*.

Few mainstream scientific studies have thus far been conducted on the strange substance. But even if a tenth of what proponents of White Gold say is true, the potential for humanity is remarkable.

Preliminary studies have shown it to assist in a variety of diverse fields including agriculture, engineering and aeronautics. For example, small studies have been conducted by universities to evaluate Ormus' effects on various fruits and vegetables, and the results are impressive. Farmers and growers worldwide have also reported increased growth in crops, nuts, fruits and vegetables as a result of using Ormus.

Of course, it's the superconductor's effects on the human brain that we shall concentrate on in this chapter. Aiding memory, assisting mental wellbeing, helping students achieve better grades, improving eyesight and correcting damaged DNA are but a few of the astonishing claims surrounding the substance.

Ormus test results are apparently off the charts and defy the laws of science. White Gold experts explain this by saying the substance exists in the realms of quantum physics and hyperdimensional theory. Skeptics, however, say Ormus more appropriately exists in the twilight zone and its benefits are nowhere near conclusively proven.

Consumers of the little known substance, which is created in different forms by hundreds of commercial manufacturers worldwide, come from all sectors of society. Examples range from elite athletes looking for legal performance-enhancers to terminally ill people seeking alternative cures for illnesses modern medicine cannot cure to Fortune 500 CEOs attempting to get a mental advantage over competitors; A-List

Hollywood stars are also among those who regularly ingest Ormus.

DISCOVERY

Ormus was discovered in 1975 by David Hudson (Figure 22), an Arizona cotton farmer and wealthy businessman. Hudson came across the substance while conducting analysis of natural resources on one of his farms in Arizona. He ended up devoting his life and millions of dollars to researching the strange substance, which he linked to Biblical and ancient Egyptian alchemy.

It was an unusual-looking white powder that the farmer discovered by chance. When he put the powder out to dry in the hot Arizona sun, it radically changed – from powder to oil!

After conducting scientific analysis of the substance, Hudson confirmed it seems to have odd properties that defy the laws of nature. For example, Ormus' elements, which include gold, copper and iron, frequently morph into other elements and the substance becomes an electromagnetic superconductor under certain conditions.

Hudson claimed to have knowledge of secretive Government-funded studies of Ormus. He said these experiments took place in laboratories throughout the US and in the Soviet Union in the 1980's.

If such experiments did take place, they've never been made public.

In the late 1980's, Hudson was issued a British patent by the UK Intellectual Property Office for the Ormus product he formulated from his initial discovery. At the same time, he coined a term for the exotic elements he patented – *Orbitally Rearranged Monoatomic Elements*, or *ORME*.

Shortly thereafter, Hudson was informed he no longer had the patent. He claims no clear reason was given and, soon after that setback, he received a visit from the US Department of Defense.

Hudson then enigmatically became reclusive and made few if any public appearances for about 20 years. Nor did he make any comments about Ormus during that period. Only in the last two to three years has he ventured into the public arena again, giving lectures about his discovery.

It's worth considering the following excerpt by Barry Carter – arguably the world's foremost expert on Ormus and one of the few who personally knows David Hudson – from an article Carter wrote on the subtleenergies.com website: "It is my firm belief that, once it becomes widely known, the discovery of the ORMUS materials will be heralded as the greatest scientific discovery in human history."

SCIENTIFIC PROPERTIES

Ormus is a complex concentrate of chemical elements. Besides gold, it contains a number of other metals including rhodium, iridium, copper and platinum. These metals are said to exist in the monoatomic state, or *m-state* – an unusual high-spin state of matter where metals don't form bonds or crystals but remain single atoms.

Incidentally, Ormus' non-scientific name White Powder Gold refers to the fact that when processed its appearance is reminiscent of cocaine powder.

M-state elements are naturally abundant in seawater, and the pure sea salt in seawater is said to be responsible for these rare, high-spin particles. Ormus' properties are also said to be present in most rocks as well as in trees.

In addition, various researchers have independently claimed to have found Ormus elements embedded in the DNA structure of animals and plants as well as in humans' skin, nails, hair, blood, brain and, indeed, in all the organs.

Different methods for obtaining Ormus elements have been devised in recent years – the easiest and most common of which involves combining ocean water, lye water and distilled water in the right fashion. This method is said to be so simple it can be done by anyone in their own home.

Figure 22: *David Hudson giving a lecture on Ormus.*

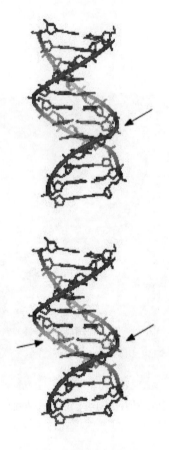

Figure 23: *Single stranded and double stranded damage to DNA*

"Ssvsds" Licensed under CC BY-SA 3.0 via Wikimedia Commons

Supposed formulas, or *recipes*, have been posted on various websites online. However, it's not clear whether these formulas lead to the same Ormus elements as those David Hudson discovered.

CLAIMS OF INTELLIGENCE BENEFITS

As mentioned, Ormus is often taken in an attempt to improve a person's intelligence and overall brain health. In its powdered form, it's usually ingested sublingually, or under the tongue. When taken this way, it goes straight into the bloodstream, which affects the body's entire system, including the brain. Alternatively, in its liquid state, White Gold can be drunk as a potion or else applied topically to the skin.

Not long after he discovered Ormus and began analyzing it, David Hudson said the substance could repair the body on a genetic level. Proponents also say the substance can correct errors in the DNA (Figure 23) and even activate Junk DNA.

Lt. Lawrence F. Frego, who wrote about Ormus' positive impact on human intelligence in his book *An End To All Disease*, agrees with this theory.

"Our very brain tissue itself is by dry weight, composed of 5% monatomic iridium and rhodium. The implications for creating a few geniuses or treating brain dysfunctions are immense. Ormus iridium affects the pituitary gland in a way that reactivates the body's Junk DNA and underused parts of the brain. Feeling stupid today? Take a little iridium and rhodium and call me in the morning. Colloidal gold has been proven to raise I.Q. by 20 points in 30 days. Certainly the thing to have for finals week."

Elsewhere in the book Lt. Frego states, "Monatomic gold and the platinum group metals dismantle incorrect DNA and rebuilds the DNA again, correctly. They activate the endocrine system and pineal gland in a way that heightens awareness and aptitude to extraordinary levels."

Lt. Frego goes on to surmise that Ormus also causes increased melatonin from the pineal gland, which can result in, among other things, better sleep, heightened alertness and many other mental benefits.

It's worth mentioning that most commercial manufacturers of Ormus have numerous testimonials from customers. Testimonials on the manufacturers' websites claim cures for all sorts of serious illnesses, including mental disorders, diabetes, heart disease and osteoporosis. Various anti-aging results have also been reported.

Again, though, it should be stressed none of these mental benefits or any other health benefits have been conclusively proven scientifically. It's anybody's guess whether satisfied Ormus users experienced the placebo effect or whether there simply haven't been enough mainstream studies conducted to support users' claims.

Only time will tell.

HOLLYWOOD STARS ON ORMUS

Since its discovery, White Gold has been used by a raft of Hollywood stars. It's especially popular with middle-aged starlets – not surprising given the substance's purported anti-aging benefits and the fact Hollywood is notorious for casting young, or at least youthful-looking, actresses for most major roles.

But it may also be the intelligence-boosting claims that have attracted certain film stars to the substance.

Gwyneth Paltrow (Figure 24)is probably the most vocal Ormus user in the Hollywood community. On the website alchemicalelixirs.com a testimonial (of hers) appears as follows:

Gwyneth Paltrow said: August 10th, 2009 5:27 pm

Dear Brendan, congratulations on your wonderful website, I must admit I am a little bit jealous that our little secret about your incredible ORMUS is now available to the world. I know I can't stand in the way of human evolution and I am proud of you for your part in raising awareness and the planets

Figure 24: *Gwyneth Paltrow enthusiastic about Ormus*

"Gwyneth Paltrow avp Iron Man 3 Paris" by Georges Biard - Own work.

Licensed under CC BY-SA 3.0 via Wikimedia Commons

consciousness through your ORMUS, god bless you, love Gwyneth x PS can you send me another few bottles of your latest brew my stash is running low thanks xx

Alchemical Elixirs, which also lists Jennifer Aniston and Audrey Tautou among its clients, is just one of many Ormus manufacturers and suppliers that names film stars, business executives, top sportsmen and famous musicians among its customers.

"They claimed that it (Ormus) perfects the cells of the body. Well I can show you tomorrow Bristol-Myers-Squib research that shows that this material inter-reacts with DNA, correcting the DNA. All the carcinogenic damage, all the radiation damage, all is corrected from these elements in the presence of the cell."

~ David Hudson

For around US$100 or less you can try Ormus for yourself by ordering it direct from any one of the various commercial enterprises that manufacture or supply it. It appears the manufacturers all use different formulas and, in the tradition of alchemists, those formulas for the most part seem to remain secret.

Any mainstream studies into Ormus will be worth keeping an eye on.

For the time-being, however, the substance remains shrouded in mystery and it's very hard to find the truth amongst the hype. This task is not made any easier with all the quasi-science commercial manufacturers are using to support their claims. No doubt the composition of their products is far removed from the properties of farmer Hudson's original discovery.

If you are thinking of purchasing a batch of Ormus, there are a couple of things to keep in mind. Besides the stunning testimonials surrounding White Gold, it's worth noting numerous users have also reported taking it and noticing no tangible results.

So it's a case of buyer beware and *always consult your doctor*.

12

SENSORY DEPRIVATION

"I think it's one of the most incredible pieces of equipment for self-help and introspective thought that you could ever find."

~ Joe Rogan quoted in an Oct. 12, 2012
article in The Atlantic

In *The Orphan Factory*, the children in our fictional orphanage receive some of their education in enclosed flotation tanks, also known as isolation tanks.

Floating inside isolation tanks is a type of sensory deprivation – or *sendep* for short – which is another genius learning technique.

Sendep is achieved by reducing or completely removing stimuli from one or more senses. Certain brain glands, such as the pineal gland, are known to become more active in this state of reduced sensory perception.

Isolation tanks (Figure 25) were invented in 1954 by American physician and neuroscientist John C. Lilly as a way to test the effects of sensory deprivation on the brain and also study the origin of consciousness itself.

Lilly proved that brainwaves are considerably altered while in this deeply relaxed state, making the floating participants very receptive to new information.

The ingredients of isolation tank sessions are simply water and salt, and the individual floats alone for about an hour inside the lightless, soundproof tank. The experience has been likened by many to being inside the womb.

Celebrities known to have used such flotation tanks include Robin Williams, John Lennon, Jeff Bridges, Joe Rogan and Susan Sarandon.

William Hurt, the star of *Altered States* – a 1980 feature film based on Paddy Chayefsky's novel of the same name and loosely inspired by John C. Lilly's isolation tank experiments – is another celebrity said to have practiced sensory deprivation in his private life.

Various sports teams, including the Philadelphia Eagles and the Dallas Cowboys have also used flotation tanks, as have

Figure 25: *A modern isolation tank*
"Flotation Tank Isolation Tank" by Floatguru - Own work.
Licensed under CC BY-SA 3.0 via Wikimedia Commons

Figure 26: *Yoshiro Nakamatsu (中松 義郎), aka Dr. NakaMats.*

"Nakamatsu" by Ushuaia.pl - Own work.

Licensed under CC BY-SA 3.0 via Wikimedia Commons

Olympians such as American track star and nine-time gold medal-winner Carl Lewis.

You'll recall how in earlier chapters we mentioned that the subconscious mind can be accessed more readily when individuals operate in less common brainwaves such as alpha, theta, delta or gamma.

Well, numerous studies have shown that during flotation tank sessions a transition from everyday beta brainwaves to alpha and theta brainwaves nearly always occurs in participants. Such brainwaves are usually only accessible just before, during or after sleep, or otherwise whilst in deep meditation.

Being in the theta brainwave is known to be extremely conducive to *super learning* as well as stimulating other positive interrelated effects such as problem solving, achieving emotional stability and heightened creativity.

Studies have also shown the more regularly a participant does flotation tank sessions, the longer the theta brainwaves last during and after a session.

In the early 1990's, research conducted at Ohio State University showed that flotation sessions improve accuracy in rifle shooting, creativity in musicians and concentration in students before exams.

Research in Europe has also shown significant reductions in stress levels are achieved by regular *floaters*.

However, floating in isolation tanks is just one way to achieve sensory deprivation.

The raw equivalent of flotation sessions is often carried out in scientific laboratories where subjects lie on a bed in a totally dark room with no sound. Even more basic forms of sendep can be achieved with the use of simple items such as hoods, earplugs or blindfolds.

We should also note (but not recommend!) other more extreme forms of sendep do exist. These include food deprivation, torture techniques and even methods that involve putting one's life at risk such as *breath play* . . . Yes, as in the BDSM technique that employs oxygen starvation to increase sexual pleasure by making other senses more sensitive.

A March 2, 2014 article published on the *Listverse* site, listing secret habits of geniuses, mentions an additional and highly unusual form of sendep.

The writer reports that Japanese inventor Dr. Yoshiro Nakamatsu, who prefers to be called Sir Dr. NakaMats (Figure 26), uses an obscure and dangerous sendep technique to receive ideas for his greatest inventions. These (inventions) include his revolutionary creation of the floppy disk in 1952.

The article states, "Many of his greatest ideas hit him when he was close to drowning. Dr. NakaMats believes in the mental benefits of long, airless stints underwater."

Dr. NakaMats is quoted as saying, "To starve the brain of oxygen, you must dive deep and allow the water pressure to deprive the brain of blood. Zero-point-five seconds before death, I visualize an invention."

The eccentric inventor apparently writes down his ideas on a notepad underwater before swimming back to the surface.

It goes without saying, we definitely don't recommend trying this form of sendep!

13

THE HIGH-IQ DIET

What you eat can definitely influence your intelligence, studies have universally shown. This is especially true for increasing the IQ of children.

A 2011 article headed *Food for thought – diet does boost your intelligence,* by Richard Alleyne, Science Correspondent for UK newspaper *The Telegraph,* confirms that "Children brought up on healthy diets are more intelligent compared with their junk food eating counterparts, new research suggests."

The article states, "Toddlers fed a diet packed high in fats, sugars, and processed foods had lower IQs than those fed pasta, salads and fruit, it was found. The effect is so great that researchers from the University of Bristol said those children with a "healthier" diet may get an IQ boost.

"Scientists stressed good diet was vital in a child's early life as the brain grows at its fastest rate during the first three years of life."

Children fed breast milk have also been shown to develop higher IQ's.

Docosahexaenoic acid (DHA), for example, is an omega-3 fatty acid found in breast milk, and a lack of DHA hinders brain development.

Large quantities of the fatty acid Lauric Acid are also found in breast milk and this, too, has major benefits for developing brains.

Breast milk is a wonderfully complex substance and scientists are still trying to figure out how exactly it has so many benefits for children's brains.

However, it's not just children who can increase their IQ's with diet. Adults can, too.

Research has shown that certain foods, herbs and natural supplements can sharpen memory, lift mental performance and generally boost brain power.

These beneficial dietary items include:

- Leafy greens and orange-red fruits and vegetables such as apricots, mangoes, red peppers and spinach, which all boost brain function as a result of their

Figure 27: Brain food

*"Fruits vegetables and nuts" by Scott Bauer,
U.S. Department of Agriculture*

Licensed under Public Domain via Wikimedia Commons

antioxidants and beta carotene properties.

- Certain organic breakfast cereals – especially those fortified with folic acid – have many mental benefits.

- Fresh seafood has a beneficial impact on the brain as a result of the biochemical roles played by the omega-3 fats and zinc content.

- Nuts and seeds have essential fatty acids and phospho-lipids that aid brain nerve cells.

- Protein-rich foods contain large amounts of the brain chemical dopamine, which increases mental alertness.

- Ginkgo Biloba is a herb that improves blood flow to the brain and has been proven to be a valid way to increase memory and concentration powers.

- Phosphatidylserine (PS) is a chemical compound that has been shown to assist with learning, focus and memory.

- Vinpocetine is a plant extract that's a cerebral vasodilator – meaning it widens blood vessels in the brain and allows more blood to enter the head for oxygenation to occur. The result is greater mental alertness. Recent studies indicate Vinpocetine may also be one of the most powerful memory enhancers on the planet.

General rules for eating for brain optimization include:

- Rather than eating one or two large meals, consume regular small meals throughout the day as this has positive psychological effects.

- Eat enough carbohydrates as the brain needs glucose to function.

- Never skip breakfast, otherwise blood sugar levels will drop by late morning and this will negatively affect memory.

There's also some good news for alcohol lovers. Red wine, due to the grape content, has a protective agent called resveratrol, which scientific research has shown to stimulate brain cells. Beer can also be a brain-booster because of its high quantities of boron and B vitamins – both of which affect mental function.

However, the golden rule of *everything in moderation* definitely applies to the subject of alcohol and intelligence as overdrinking kills brain cells – never a good thing if you're already low on brain cells or are looking to increase your intelligence!

14

SMART DRUGS

In chapter 10, you'll recall we quoted Dr. Takaaki Musha as saying the mysterious superluminal (faster-than-light) particles inside the brain may be related to genius intelligence.

The former Japanese Ministry of Defense research scientist also believes certain drugs might be able to "enhance the activities of superluminal particles in the microtubules within the brain. If so, such drugs could greatly improve mental capabilities."

Dr. Musha continues, "The molecules of some drugs can change the order of microtubule polymers, which may enhance the computational capability and other capabilities of the human brain."

Some believe there is already a real-world equivalent of the brain-improving drug Bradley Cooper's character took in the 2011 Hollywood movie *Limitless*. The film's plot is about a guy of average intelligence becoming a genius and polymath overnight simply by taking a nootropic, or what's more commonly termed a *smart drug*.

Nootropics are drugs that improve various aspects of brain functions, including concentration, memory and alertness.

Officially at least, no *Limitless*-style drug exists and no consumers of nootropics are becoming geniuses overnight as they did in that film.

There are rumors, however, that smart drugs of the potency depicted in *Limitless* were formulated by chemists decades ago, but have been suppressed from the masses.

According to this conspiracy theory, classified nootropics are used by the likes of the CIA and various splinter groups of the global elite to turn spies and key political figures into extremely high IQ individuals. Sounds a bit far-fetched, we know, and possibly it is.

On the other hand, considering the well-documented and declassified mind control programs such as MK-Ultra, using suppressed intelligence enhancers on persons of interest seems rather benign by comparison – and very feasible as well.

Furthermore, any scientific breakthrough involving revolutionary smart drugs would likely be suppressed from the mainstream – at least within the parameters of such theories.

The 2012 film *The Bourne Legacy*, which stars Jeremy Renner and Rachel Weisz and was directed by Tony Gilroy, shows the CIA improving their operatives' effectiveness by altering their DNA with top-secret drugs. Weisz plays a CIA chemist employed to design the drugs that make Renner's character and other operatives physically and intellectually superior to average humans.

Are the plots behind such films pure fiction or are they inspired by real goings-on in the world of intelligence agencies and classified science?

The reason for mentioning this whole conspiracy theory is not to go off on some unrelated tangent without purpose or to explore something that is not practical for those wanting to become geniuses. Rather, we bring the subject up to assess whether science (not just official science but all forms of science including *classified* science) has already evolved to the point where highly sophisticated smart drugs have been formulated.

And if that is indeed the truth of the matter, then perhaps it's possible for the layman to get access to such drugs – over the counter or perhaps on the black market – by purchasing little-known products or even creating exotic drugs themselves from raw ingredients.

One smart drug manufacturer, who we shall call XYZ so as not to inadvertently advertise their products or company, implies that there is a conspiracy in place whereby the FDA block the most advanced nootropics from reaching the public in a concerted effort to make sure Americans never get too intelligent!

"The official reason is 'to keep the public safe'—this is the standard excuse given for police-state behavior," according to XYZ's website. "A more plausible explanation might be to keep the public from becoming too smart. A smarter public would be less tolerant of corrupt and incompetent government officials."

Notwithstanding the theory of suppressed or classified smart drugs being withheld from the public, there's already an impressive list of FDA-approved smart drugs freely available to Jo Public. And many users swear by them. Positive testimonials about such drugs range from customers claiming they achieved better results in exams to making more money in business and wiser decision-making in their personal lives.

IQ-enhancing drugs are nothing new. Italian neurobiologist Rita Levi-Montalcini (1909-2012), who received the 1986 Nobel Prize in Physiology or Medicine for her discovery of nerve growth factor, was said to be an early proponent of a smart drug. Some attribute Levi-

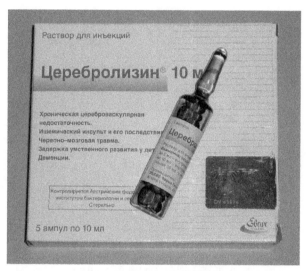

Figure 28: *A Russian manufactured version of the nootropic Cerebrolysin*

"Cerebrolysin" by chan - Own work. Licensed under Public Domain via Wikimedia Commons

Figure 29: *DARPA . . . conspiring against The People?*

"DARPA Logo" by DARPA - DARPA.mil.

Licensed under Public Domain via Wikimedia Commons

Montalcini's longevity (she lived to 103) and her ongoing mental sharpness to her daily routine of applying the very chemical she discovered to her eyes each morning.

And, of course, caffeine is a nootropic most people already use on a daily basis to fire up the brain.

Now smart drugs are widely available, and the masses are starting to catch on to this big-time – so intense is the hunger for such intelligence-enhancers.

For example, the term *academic doping* is starting to achieve mainstream awareness – and for good reason. Academic doping, which is the educational equivalent of sports doping, is on the rise and students on smart drugs are said to be achieving better grades.

Numerous studies have shown around 5-10% of North American students and 1-5% of European students have used smart drugs to assist them with their studies. These statistics are likely to only increase as places in learning institutions become more competitive and expensive for prospective students.

Popular nootropics used in high schools and on university campuses all over the world include modafinil, dimethylamylamine and methylphenidate. Neurotransmitters like GABA and plant extracts such as vinpocetine, bacoside A and huperzine A are also commonly used by students because of the potential of these nootropic substances.

These intelligence-boosting and neuro-enhancing drugs and stimulants have been scientifically proven to increase productivity, memory and overall cognitive functioning.

In the June 16, 2014 edition of the academic journal *The Conversation*, an article on smart drugs co-written by Georgia State University neuroscience associate professor Nicole A. Vincent points out that "all around the world, students, academics and professionals of various stripes are increasingly experimenting with new cognitive enhancement technologies to boost their memory, attention, reflexes, clarity of thought and ability to function well with little sleep.

"Several recent studies," the article continues, "report around a 30% improvement in language learning by subjects who used modafinil."

Many of the intelligence-enhancing effects of smart drugs may relate to the importance of activating dormant areas of the brain, as mentioned in earlier chapters of this book. For example, the experimental drug NSI-189 has been shown to stimulate neural pathways in the hippocampus.

Incidentally, research into NSI-189 has been primarily funded by the Defense Advanced Research Projects Agency (DARPA) (Figure 29), which possibly supports the suspicion that the powers-that-be are researching smart drugs and using them in classified experiments.

Another drug compound called dihexa has been shown in laboratory experiments to build new neural connections in rats and mice and also to repair brain damage.

A July 29, 2014 article by the BBC headlined *The truth about smart drugs* covers the pros and cons of synthetic intelligence-enhancers and asks whether the *Limitless* (movie) scenario really is possible. Although fairly pessimistic overall, the article mentions that Gary Lynch, a professor in the School of Medicine at the University of California, "argues that recent advances in neuroscience have opened the way for the smart design of drugs, configured for specific biological targets in the brain."

The article also quotes Lynch as saying memory enhancement is not very far off although the prospects for other kinds of mental enhancement are "very difficult to know . . . To me, there's an inevitability to the thing, but a timeline is difficult."

The BBC report continues, "In the nearer future, Lynch points to nicotinic receptor agents – molecules that act on the neurotransmitter receptors affected by nicotine – as ones to watch when looking out for potential new cognitive enhancers."

So while nobody has been documented as becoming an outright genius after taking such drugs, it may not be far off before such an occurrence is official and on the record.

15

MEDITATION & YOGA

Meditation is proven to be a very effective way to boost mind power.

Brain scans on long-term meditators have consistently shown parts of their brains have been activated that haven't been (activated) in other individuals. And they are more regularly in the relaxing alpha and theta brain waves than non-meditators.

Some successful and famous long-time meditators who use Transcendental Meditation (TM) and other similar meditation techniques include Hugh Jackman, Ellen DeGeneres, Rupert Murdoch, Oprah Winfrey (Figure 30), Katy Perry, Howard Stern, Russell Brand, Jerry

Figure 30: *Oprah a dedicated meditator.*
"Oprah closeup" by Alan Light - Flickr.
Licensed under CC BY 2.0 via Wikimedia Commons

Seinfeld, Martin Scorsese and Sir Paul McCartney.

Another famous meditator is American film director and author David Lynch who often mentions the importance of TM in his life when speaking in public. In his 2006 book *Catching the Big Fish*, Lynch talks about the wells of creativity this form of meditation allowed him to access.

"Meditation is all about the pursuit of nothingness. It's like the ultimate rest. It's better than the best sleep you've ever had. It's a quieting of the mind. It sharpens everything, especially your appreciation of your surroundings. It keeps life fresh."

~ Hugh Jackman

Yoga may also hold great potential for intelligence, although there have been limited studies done on this complex subject to date. One body of research was covered in an article by IQ test experts headlined *Yoga Enhances IQ*.

"Clinical tests have shown," the article begins, "that consistent yoga practice can raise your IQ and increase your memory. Studies have found that yoga, besides improving fitness, health, co-ordination, reaction time and memory, also positively influences IQ.

"The brain functions of attention, cognition, processing of sensory information and visual perception are honed with yogic practices. Yogic practices – like hatha yoga, which is a medley of asanas, pranayama, meditation and Om chanting – increase blood feed to the brain. This helps in soothing the mind and enhances concentration. Memory power is given a boost, while also improving the ability to maintain focus and concentration."

A renowned genius who has perhaps influenced as many lives as any other creative thinker in the modern era was Apple co-founder Steve Jobs (1955-2011) (Figure 31). Although the history of his illustrious career in the tech industry has been well documented in books, movies and untold news articles, few are aware that Jobs was intensely interested in Yoga.

Yoga Journal published an article on September 11, 2013 about the master inventor's lifelong relationship with the Eastern discipline.

"Steve Jobs will long be remembered as an innovator whose vision changed the way we interact with the world through technology. But what many people don't know is that Jobs was guided by an intense interest in spirituality and yoga."

In 1974, shortly after he had dropped out of college, Jobs traveled to India as a backpacker. He stayed on the the subcontinent for seven months and during this period he first discovered and began to practice Yoga. He cited

Figure 31: *Yoga enthusiast Steve Jobs introduces his iPad creation.*

"Steve Jobs with the Apple iPad no logo" by matt buchanan - originally posted to Flickr as Apple iPad Event.

Licensed under CC BY 2.0 via Wikimedia Commons

Figure 32: *Jobs unveils his iPhone 4 invention*
"Steve Jobs Headshot 2010-CROP" by Matthew Yohe
Licensed under CC BY-SA 3.0 via Wikimedia Commons

the experiences he had of meeting Yogis at ashrams all over India as being among the most influential of his life.

The 19 year-old returned to the US an altogether different person. Two years later, in 1976, Jobs co-founded Apple (with fellow college dropout Steve Wozniak) after having the revolutionary idea of personal computing for the masses.

Some say that Jobs' statement "I was worth over $1,000,000 when I was 23, and over $10,000,000 when I was 24, and over $100,000,000 when I was 25, and it wasn't that important because I never did it for the money," was directly inspired by this passage from the holy Indian scripture *Bhagavad Gita*: "Relinquishing attachment to the fruits of work, always contented, independent (of material rewards), the wise do not perform any (binding) action even in the midst of activities."

Whether that's true or not is open to conjecture, but reportedly, the only book Jobs ever downloaded to his iPad was *Autobiography of a Yogi*, by Paramahansa Yogananda (Figure 33).

And in a 2013 interview with CNET.com, Marc Benioff, former business associate and close friend of Jobs, said guests at the iPhone/iPad/iPod creator's memorial service were "each given a copy of the classic book *Autobiography of a Yogi* as per Jobs' wishes."

Figure 33: *Steve Jobs' favorite book*
"Autobiography-of-a-Yogi" by Tat Sat - Own work.
Licensed under Public Domain via Wikimedia Commons

Benioff added, "He had the incredible realization that his intuition was his greatest gift and he needed to look at the world from the inside out."

Yogic techniques for accelerated learning are probably related to other topics on the brain covered elsewhere in this book, including superluminal particles, brainwaves and the activation of dormant brain glands.

Besides meditation, breathing and posture are of course major components of most Yogic systems.

Posture being related to intelligence makes sense. After all, it seems difficult if not impossible to perform complex mental tasks while slouching, and most people automatically and unconsciously sit or stand upright and erect when faced with intellectual challenges. Good posture alone can mean scoring 5-10 points higher on an IQ test. Therefore it makes sense to maintain an erect spine at all times.

Deep breathing techniques to increase brain activity may also have some scientific validation. After all, the more oxygen you inhale, the more will enter your bloodstream and the more will be delivered to the brain, which requires rich supplies of oxygen to work efficiently.

Yogic breathing techniques, known as Pranayama, increase the supply of oxygen to the brain, which in turn enhances memory and concentration.

"One becomes firmly established in practice only after attending to it for a long time, without interruption and with an attitude of devotion."

~ *Yoga Sutra I.14*

16

MIDBRAIN ACTIVATION

*"The purpose of education in the future
will not be to create people with heads
crammed full of knowledge, but to rear
children who know how to efficiently
use the whole brain. Rearing children
with enormous ability, rich creativity,
and the capability to make use of a high
proportion of their brain should be the
goal of child rearing."*

~ *Professor Makoto Shichida*

There is a specific area of the brain known as the
mesencephalon, or more commonly referred to
as the *midbrain* (Figure 34), that some modern

educators (especially in Asia) believe can greatly enhance intelligence when fully activated.

In recent years, millions of children in India, China, Malaysia and Singapore have been enrolled in schools that specialize in activating their midbrains. Such radical learning institutions are reportedly churning out geniuses by the veritable truckload.

These schools claim to teach pupils how to learn rapidly and study almost effortlessly. This is apparently achieved by absorbing tremendous amounts of knowledge via their midbrains instead of the cerebral cortex where most humans think from.

The Mumbai-based news media outlet DNA India ran an article on August 5, 2014 headed *Make superkids through midbrain activation in Mumbai centres.*

"Want your child to be a super kid?" the article begins. "Get him midbrain-activated. That's what the latest child development programme in town is advising parents. At least 20 centres of the 'midbrain activation programme' have already come up across the country."

In line with most of the techniques and technologies mentioned throughout this book, the article states that "Midbrain-activation experts say the trick lies in the equal use of right and left sides of the brain."

The theory behind creating geniuses in this fashion is about optimizing the middle brain,

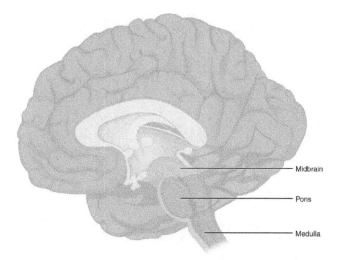

Midbrain

Pons

Medulla

Figure 34: *The Midbrain (mesencephalon) near the center of the brain*

"1311 Brain Stem" by OpenStax College - Anatomy & Physiology, Connexions Web site.

http://cnx.org/content/col11496/1.6/ Jun 19, 2013. Licensed under CC BY 3.0 via Wikimedia Commons

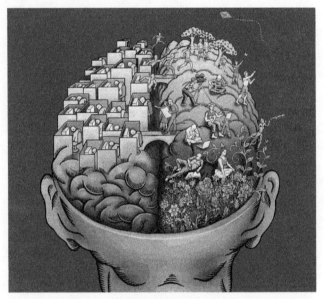

Figure 35: *The Right Brain is the more creative hemisphere.*

"Right brain" by Allan Ajifo

Licensed under CC BY 2.0 via Wikimedia Commons

which connects the left and right brain. Building a bridge like this between both brains apparently allows easy exchanges of information, which in turn allows for smooth and efficient learning.

The end result of midbrain activation is said to be a brain that functions as a whole rather than having the usual division between left and right hemispheres (of the brain).

According to the DNA India article, "Midbrain activation experts claim they can enhance imagination power, intuition and super intelligence among children in the age bracket of 5-15 years."

And it's not just children whose midbrains can be activated via such methods. Adults are also apparently accessing untapped reservoirs of mental capabilities.

Abilities of those who have fully activated their midbrains are said to include photographic memory, performing complex mental calculations, mastering foreign languages in rapid time, speed-reading and even converting images to words, numbers and symbols in their minds.

Studies have consistently shown that around 80% of the world's population have a more developed left brain.

So what are most of us missing out on by having an underutilized right brain? (Figure 35)

A lot, according to the experts!

An article by Taiwanese magazine *Sinorama*, titled *Waking the Right Brain –A new approach to pre-school education*, is enlightening on this issue. It mentions that "the right brain is believed to possess extraordinary powers which have their origins in instincts which pre-date education and civilization."

The article continues, "As early as 1975, brain specialists had discovered that the cerebral cortex, unique to primates, was responsible for intellectual activities such as language and reasoning. The limbic system lies below the cortex and pre-dates it. Sometimes called the mammalian brain, it is involved in the expression of emotions. On the lowest level lies the brain stem, sometimes called the reptilian brain. It controls basic bodily functions such as breathing and heartbeat."

Many intelligence researchers believe these older, more primitive parts of the brain, especially in the midbrain section, are where genius abilities come from.

As in-depth studies on stimulating this part of the brain have yet to be conducted, it remains to be seen whether geniuses can be created via midbrain activation. Meanwhile, more and more students in Asia continue to swear by the method.

"The Midbrain can put us in the creative domain in no time at all."

~ Dr. Baskaran Pillai

17

HYPNOTISM

"Cus (D'Amato) used to have me professionally hypnotized two or three times a day – before sparring, before training and before fights."

~ Mike Tyson. From a 2013 interview with UK newspaper the Daily Telegraph.

Another way to achieve accelerated learning and optimum mental performance is hypnotism – a technique that has been shown in many scientific studies to prime the mind for intense concentration.

Hypnotism has been used by countless renowned figures spanning numerous fields of expertise. They include Albert Einstein.

The German-born theoretical physicist was known to do hypnosis sessions every afternoon. Einstein's great *theory of relativity* discovery entered his mind during one of those sessions, and he used the hypnotic trance state to develop many of his other theories and formulas.

American inventor Thomas Edison used hypnotism on a regular basis – self-hypnosis in fact.

In Britain, Princess Diana utilized hypnosis to improve her public speaking skills, while Sir Winston Churchill was given post-hypnotic suggestions so he could stave off tiredness and endure long periods without sleep throughout WW2.

Several great classical music composers were hypnotism devotees. They include Seigei Rachmaninoff who, after a post-hypnotic suggestion given by early hypnosis specialist Nikolai Dahl, composed his much loved *Second Piano Concerto*; Mozart (Figure 36) also used hypnotism as a creative aid and his opera *Cosi Fan Tutte* was entirely composed in a hypnotic trance.

Nineteenth Century British poet Lord Alfred Tennyson was known to regularly write poems in a hypnotic state.

Figure 36: *Mozart . . . An early adopter of hypnosis*

"Wolfgang-amadeus-mozart 1" by Barbara Krafft - Deutsch, Otto Erich (1965)

Mozart: A Documentary Biography. Stanford: Stanford University Press

Licensed under Public Domain via Wikimedia Commons

Figure 37: *Michael "Air" Jordan hypnotized before every game*

"Jordan by Lipofsky 16577" by Steve Lipofsky
www.Basketballphoto.com

Licensed under CC BY-SA 3.0 via Wikimedia Commons

While writing the feature film screenplay of *Rocky*, the then-unknown Sylvester Stallone used self-hypnosis tapes to boost willpower and creativity. Later, during each day of filming *Rocky*, in 1975, Stallone worked with well-regarded hypnotherapist Gil Boyne to help ensure the movie would become the blockbuster it turned out to be.

While writing the feature film screenplay of *Rocky*, the then-unknown Sylvester Stallone used self-hypnosis tapes to boost willpower and creativity. Later, during each day of filming *Rocky*, in 1975, Stallone worked with well-regarded hypnotherapist Gil Boyne to help ensure the movie would become the blockbuster it turned out to be.

Continuing with the boxing theme, in Mike Tyson's 2013 autobiography *Undisputed Truth*, Tyson mentions how he used hypnotism and self-hypnotism throughout his career, and specifically before each fight. He partly attributes this to his success in becoming a two-time World Heavyweight champion.

Tyson cites French psychologist Émile Coué's self-hynotism methods, including autosuggestion, as being amongst those he used.

Coué's 1922 book *Self-Mastery Through Conscious Autosuggestion* is recommended further reading on the subject of self-hypnotism.

Another famous athlete to use hypnosis for sports performance is Tiger Woods. The man who is arguably the greatest golfer of all time has been practicing hypnosis – both with a hypnotist and giving himself hypnotic suggestions – since his early teens. This period of his life was also when he started his extensive *mental training* with family friend and psychologist Dr. Jay Brunza.

Besides Tyson and Woods, another major sports star to have regularly used hypnosis during his career was Michael Jordan (Figure 37). The basketball legend was hypnotized before every game to enhance his mental focus. Furthermore, the entire Chicago Bulls team, which won six NBA championships during Jordan's reign of supremacy in the 1990's, incorporated hypnotherapy in their pregame routine to gain a psychological advantage over their opponents.

SUBLIMINAL EDUCATION

Closely aligned with hypnosis are subliminal messages, which the latest research suggests may also have the potential to instruct the subconscious mind and access higher intelligence. Indeed, some hypnotists have been known to incorporate subliminal messages in hypnotic audio recordings made for clients or the public at large.

Subliminal messages – also known as *subliminals* – are probably more controversial and slightly less proven than hypnosis, however.

Subliminal messages – also known as *subliminals* – are probably more controversial and slightly less proven than hypnosis, however.

Subliminals are any sensory stimuli that occur below an individual's threshold of conscious awareness. What this means is messages can be sent to your mind without you being aware of the fact.

Subliminal messaging is nothing new of course. The technique has been around at least since the advent of radio and television when subliminal advertising reared its ugly head, and by the late 20th Century a whole host of scientific studies had concluded subliminals were not remotely effective.

However, more recent studies have shown the reverse. Science may be beginning to show just how effective subliminals can be.

For example, new studies involving *functional magnetic resonance imaging* (fMRI) have revealed that subliminals activate crucial regions of the brain including the hippocampus, the amygdala, the primary visual cortex and the insular cortex.

18

OTHER GENIUS METHODS

"For nearly a century, the science of the mind (psychology) developed independently from the science of the brain (neuroscience). Psychologists were interested in our mental functions and capacities -- how we learn, remember, and think. Neuroscientists were interested in how the brain develops and functions. It was as if psychologists were interested only in our mental software and neuroscientists only in our neural hardware. Deeply held theoretical assumptions in both fields supported a view that mind and brain could, and

indeed should, be studied independently. It is only in the past 15 years or so that these theoretical barriers have fallen. Now scientists called cognitive neuroscientists are beginning to study how our neural hardware might run our mental software, how brain structures support mental functions, how our neural circuits enable us to think and learn. This is an exciting and new scientific endeavor, but it is also a very young one. As a result we know relatively little about learning, thinking, and remembering at the level of brain areas, neural circuits, or synapses; we know very little about how the brain thinks, remembers, and learns."

~ John T. Bruer, from his 2006 essay In Search of . . . Brain-Based Education

In addition to the genius techniques mentioned in this book's preceding chapters, there are numerous other advanced learning methods. Some have been proven to work to varying degrees while others remain theoretical or speculative in nature.

In this chapter we shall focus on eight additional techniques we believe may hold brain boosting potential for aspiring geniuses.

AMBIDEXTERITY

While researching geniuses for this book we were surprised to come across the following fact:

Many of history's most renowned geniuses – scientific and artistic giants such as Albert Einstein, Michelangelo, Nikola Tesla and Leonardo da Vinci – were physically ambidextrous (or *equally* proficient with their right and left hands).

Given that less than 1% of the population are truly ambidextrous, we immediately wondered if that was just a coincidence, or was the ambidexterity of these individuals somehow crucial to the genius abilities each possessed?

Although more research needs to be done and there are some scientists who have suggested undesirable mental traits result from being ambidextrous, brain scans have revealed one telling statistic that may explain the seemingly high instance of geniuses in the ambidextrous population.

That statistic reveals that unlike *right-handers*, ambidextrous people have almost completely symmetrical brains. Meaning they are naturally in the all-important whole brain state. Right handers, on the other hand, generally have strong left brain dominance. *Lefties* often have brain symmetry as well, but not to the extent that ambidextrous people do.

You'll recall throughout this book we have referred to the whole brain mode (aka hemispheric synchronization) being the ideal state for accessing higher intelligences. So, could acquiring ambidexterity be one way of bringing out latent genius abilities?

Digging deeper, we found a *Psychology Today* article on the history and neuroscience of left-handed, right-handed and ambidextrous people. Published on August 12, 2013, and written by bestselling author and athlete Christopher Bergland, the article surmises that the ultimate state for genius-level intelligence is to create brain symmetry and to be as close as possible to ambidextrous with your hands.

Another article, published in *(e) Science News* on October 4, 2013, may also offer more specific insights. Headlined *Well-connected hemispheres of Einstein's brain may have sparked his brilliance*, the article reports that "The left and right hemispheres of Albert Einstein's (Figure 38) brain were unusually well connected to each other and may have contributed to his brilliance, according to a new study conducted in part by Florida State University evolutionary anthropologist Dean Falk."

So, if Einstein-like interconnectedness of brain hemispheres is the ultimate goal, then it seems being ambidextrous, or at least developing some ambidextrous traits, may facilitate this brain state.

Figure 38: *Albert Einstein . . . an ambidextrous genius*

"Albert Einstein (Nobel)" Official 1921 Nobel Prize in Physics photograph.

Licensed under Public Domain via Wikimedia Commons

A few techniques to develop ambidexterity include: write and draw with the wrong hand (i.e. left hand for Righties and right hand for Lefties); do household tasks with the wrong hand; play musical instruments that involve both hands such as piano, guitar or flute; learn how to juggle.

BAROQUE AND CLASSICAL MUSIC

Baroque and classical music in general – especially the (classical) works of Mozart – have been shown in some studies to aid students when learning new things or recalling information. In *The Orphan Trilogy*, we mention this form of music is played to our orphans from when they are babies in the womb right through their childhood.

The Mozart Effect: Tapping the Power of Music to Heal the Body, Strengthen the Mind, and Unlock the Creative Spirit, by Don G. Campbell, was one of the first books that introduced this idea to the masses when first published in 1997.

That book mentions scientific studies which proved that listening to specific Baroque and classical music – especially Mozart – allows humans to study and remember information better. It even mentions how a study at the University of California apparently demonstrated that this music raises IQ scores by nine points on average for subjects.

As mentioned in Chapter 8, Bulgarian psychiatrist Dr. Georgi Lozanov devised a system for rapidly learning foreign languages, using Baroque music at its core. Dr. Lazanov claimed his radical and controversial education system – called *Suggestopedia* – proved that foreign languages can be mastered in a tenth of the usual time by listening to specific Baroque pieces while learning.

Although similar studies have proven inconclusive, or even appear to contradict such claims, subscribers to this theory maintain super learning is possible with Baroque music because many recordings of this form of music have a tempo of around 60 beats per minute. The rationale is that when a person hears one beat per second of music, their heart rate and pulse relax to the beat, blood pressure decreases and the entire body unwinds. In this relaxed state, the brain is able to concentrate more easily.

An article titled *The Mozart Effect: A Closer Look*, by University of Illinois' teacher and musician Donna Lerch, mentions that Lois Hetland, of the Harvard Graduate School of Education, "attempted to replicate earlier Mozart effect studies in broader depth, including a total of 1014 subjects. Her findings were that the Mozart listening group outperformed other groups by a higher margin than could be explained by chance, although factors such as the subject's gender, musical tastes and training, innate spatial ability, and cultural background made a difference in the degree to which Mozart would increase test scores.

"Other researchers agree," the article continues, "that there are neurological foundations for music's effects on cognitive ability. John Hughes, a neurologist at the University of Illinois Medical Center in Chicago, examined hundreds of compositions and concludes that music sequences that regularly repeat every 20-30 seconds, just as Mozart's compositions do prevalently, "may trigger the strongest response in the brain, because many functions of the central nervous system such as the onset of sleep and brain wave patterns also occur in 30-second cycles.""

As mentioned though, as many studies appear to disprove the theory of Baroque and classical music aiding learning as studies that seem to prove it.

Perhaps a Southern California Public Radio (SCPR) article by reporter Mary Plummer, may explain the wild discrepancies between different studies. This article suggests familiarity and enjoyment of musical pieces is crucial to learning in this fashion.

The article states, "Peter Webster is vice dean for the Division of Scholarly and Professional Studies at USC's Thornton of Music, and he says it depends on the music — and the listener.

"Some people will find that [music] distracting," Webster is quoted in the article as saying. "Others, though, who sort of enjoy listening, let's say to a Mozart opera or something, might find putting that on in the background might in fact encourage their study skills."

"Researchers know the brain lights up when music is played," the SCPR article continues, "creative thinking and analytical processing are activated. But new music can easily distract you – stealing your brain power away from that physics study.

"But if it's a piece you know well and find soothing, Webster says it's more likely to help you take in information."

Besides Mozart, researchers claim composers whose works are most conducive to learning include Vivaldi, Bach, Pachelbel and Handel.

NLP

Neuro-linguistic programming (NLP) may be another way to increase IQ.

Created in the US in the 1970's, it is claimed there's an important link between the neurological processes ("neuro") and language ("linguistic"). The conclusion NLP makes is that desired behavioral patterns can be achieved through specific "programming."

Famous practitioners of NLP include the likes of Warren Buffet, Gerard Butler, Tony Robbins, Russell Brand, Paul McKenna and Andre Agassi.

One theory suggests it is possible to 'model genius' through NLP techniques. Modeling genius apparently requires NLP practitioners to model or adopt genius qualities they see in others they wish to be like.

For example, an aspiring professional (male) golfer may model himself on Tiger Woods, while a young businessman may model himself on Richard Branson. Or, perhaps more to the point of this book, science students could attempt to model themselves on Albert Einstein.

> ### *"The ability to concentrate is the basis for everything else."*
>
> *~ Garry Kasparov, Russian (formerly Soviet) chess grandmaster and former World Chess Champion.*

CHESS

There are references to chess throughout *The Orphan Trilogy*. Our orphans play rapid-fire matches known as *Lightning Chess* in which entire games are completed in 10 minutes or less.

This is inspired by the theory that by playing the board game from a young age, certain parts of a child's brain develop quicker than normal, especially areas relating to strategy. Playing Lightning Chess and multiple games

Figure 39: *Some studies have revealed chess positively influences children's brains.*

"Children Playing Chess on the Street - Santiago de Cuba - Cuba" by Adam Jones

Adam63 - Own work. Licensed under CC BY-SA 3.0 via Wikimedia Commons

simultaneously once again relates to thinking so fast that the conscious mind must yield to the superior subconscious.

It has been recognized by many observers that chess players often have very high IQ's and seem to exhibit many of the telltale signs of genius.

What does it do to a child's brain to play chess from a young age?

Nobody knows for sure and test results remain inconclusive to date. No doubt it is a difficult thing to study precisely given it requires studying young chess players over years if not decades.

Experimental results, however, have been collected from the likes of the Grandmaster Eugene Torre Chess Institute, in the Philippines, and the United States Chess Federation as well as other chess schools around the world. All these bodies agree that playing the board game increases intellect in young people.

Plus a few small studies have also shown that chess players develop better memories, verbal skills, mathematical abilities as well as healthier problem-solving skills and imaginations than the average person.

For example, a 1995 research study on chess and students was conducted by American cardiologist Dr. Robert Ferguson. It showed that chess improves a child's critical thinking skills. Ferguson's subjects, who were all school students aged between 11 and 14, improved their test results by 17% on average after becoming proficient chess players.

An article that appears on the neuroscience and brain health website Examined Existence provides further insights into the potential link between chess and high intelligence.

Headlined *Does Playing Chess Make You Smarter?*, the report boldly states that chess definitely improves IQ.

The article states, "According to a study conducted in Venezuela, results have shown that children who took chess classes for 4½ months have increased their IQ points. This conclusion is also backed up by a 2003 study of Murray Thompson, a Ph.D. Education student at the Flinders University in Australia. In his research, participants who played chess also demonstrated improved IQ levels. Thompson ascribes this to the concentration and logical thinking a chess game calls for."

The Examined Existence article also mentions that chess can improve mental abilities in adults as well, including the elderly. "Chess has proven to be highly effective in protecting the elderly from neuro-degenerative conditions like dementia and Alzheimer's disease."

WATER

This might fit into the *stating the bleeding obvious* category, but drinking water really can make a difference to mental alertness and overall cognitive skills.

Here's why: every time you drink water it increases the brain's electrochemical activity. Conversely, dehydration slows electrochemical activity and effectively makes you dumber.

Therefore, staying hydrated is a scientifically valid way to keep sharp mentally.

Be warned, though, drinking the right sort of water is as important as drinking enough water. And no, ordinary tap water won't do the job folks. After all, tap water usually contains high levels of fluoride.

Numerous studies have shown fluoride *reduces* IQ levels and in some cases even causes brain damage. Never a good thing for those wanting to become geniuses!

In January 2013, physician and author Dr. Joseph Mercola wrote an article for the Huffington Post titled *Harvard Study Confirms Fluoride Reduces Children's IQ*.

The article states, "A recently-published Harvard University meta-analysis funded by the National Institutes of Health (NIH) has concluded that children who live in areas with highly fluoridated water have "significantly lower" IQ scores than those who live in low fluoride areas."

The Harvard study showed that fluoride causes neurotoxicity, which negatively impacts learning and memory.

The Huffington Post article continues, "There are so many scientific studies showing the direct, toxic effects of fluoride on your body, it's truly remarkable that it's NOT considered a scientific consensus by now. Despite the evidence against it, fluoride is still added to 70 percent of U.S. public drinking water supplies."

Besides fluoride, there are a whole host of other contaminants usually found in tap water – such as chlorine and lead – and none of these will do an aspiring genius's brain any favors.

Those wishing to increase their IQ levels would be wise to only drink pure water. Filtered water (either bottled or from a home/office filtration system) is certainly better than tap water. However, contrary to what filtered water companies tell customers, their product often contains numerous impurities – sometimes as many as are found in tap water.

The only pure water available on Earth is *distilled water* (Figure 40).

As American medical doctor Dr. Andrew Weil states on his website, distilled water is "water that has been turned into steam so its impurities are left behind. The steam is then condensed to make pure water."

Dr. Weil continues, "The process of distillation kills and removes virtually all bacteria, viruses, heavy metals, and other organic and inorganic contaminants. Once distilled, the water is as pure as water can reasonably be."

It should be noted here that some health researchers believe distilled water can be detrimental to health if taken ongoing and long-term rather than for the more commonly recommended short periods or fasts. This counter theory suggests that drinking water that is completely demineralized, as is the case with distilled water, is detrimental to health in the long-run.

Dr. Weil, however, believes otherwise. He says, "While it's true that distillation removes minerals as it eliminates various other contaminants from water, I don't feel this is a problem. We get our minerals from food, not water.

"As far as acidity goes," he continues, "distilled water is close to a neutral pH and has no effect on the body's acid/base balance. Distilled water is safe to drink, and the kind of water I use myself."

If the aspiring genius hunts hard enough, bottled distilled water can be found in some supermarkets and department stores. Otherwise, water distillers can be purchased for the home.

According to our research, distilled water is likely to have the most positive effects on the brain. However, we recommend consult with your doctor first.

Figure 40: *Bottles of distilled water in Hong Kong*

"1989 HK Sheung Wan Bonham Strand VITA Distilled Water" by DWatdonSHAM

Licensed under Public Domain via Wikimedia Commons

WALKING TO EUREKA!

Another genius method that potentially falls into the "too obvious" or "too simple" category, at least on first mention, is walking.

Yes, you read that right. *Walking*.

Almost everyone has experienced wrestling with a problem all day then finally giving up and going for a stroll in the fresh air and suddenly receiving the answer unexpectedly and without trying.

Some might explain away this phenomenon as merely being the result of relaxing and defocusing from a problem and thereby allowing the subconscious mind to take over. Or others may simply say that virtually all exercise has been shown to benefit the human brain.

And there are no doubt degrees of truth to those counter points.

However, there may also be a sound scientific explanation as to why this low-impact physical exercise often yields the golden solution. Firstly, there's a rhythmic flow to walking that puts one almost in a trance-like or meditative state. Secondly, the fact that you are moving two legs and two arms means you are engaging both hemispheres of the brain – people are therefore probably in the whole brain state while walking.

One study at Stanford University showed that subjects came up with more creative ideas during and immediately after a walk compared to those who simply sat at a desk.

Furthermore, a July 31, 2014 article in *Psychology Today* mentioned that German composer and pianist Ludwig van Beethoven "kept his creative promises by strategically using his time to incubate ideas. His favorite method of thinking things through? Long, solitary walks through the forested valleys of Vienna . . . Beethoven went for a vigorous walk after lunch, and he always carried a pencil and a couple of sheets of paper in his pocket to record chance musical thoughts."

And it appears Beethoven is not alone among history's great geniuses.

Albert Einstein took long walks around Princeton University when pondering complex equations. He often commented that many of his Eureka moments and creative breakthroughs came to him during these walks.

For those who find walking too boring or just not their cup of tea, other physical exercises could possibly deliver similar results – exercises such as dancing, cycling or running for example.

Athletes, personal fitness trainers and sports medicine professionals are united in their opinion that exercise helps your mental function. Runners experience the pleasant – many say euphoric – *runner's high* that comes with intense, sustained exercise. Such exercise (not just running) increases serotonin in the brain, leading to improved mental clarity.

PERIPHERAL VISION

Peripheral vision is what we use when something catches our attention "out of the corner of our eye." It is the opposite of central vision, which is literally the center of our vision (looking directly ahead) (Figure 41).

Most people in the modern world use central vision all day long with narrow field activities – such as looking at computer screens, reading books and watching television. This is akin to tunnel vision.

By contrast, our ancestors (especially Early Man) had stronger or better-attuned peripheral vision as they were primarily engaged in outdoor activities such as hunting, fishing, fighting and traveling. To survive, they needed to scan entire landscapes to spot enemies and predatory animals and the like.

In cinematic terms, our modern vision would be a close-up or extreme close-up whereas Early Man's vision was akin to a panoramic wide-angle shot.

The problem with central vision is it has been shown in studies to be directly linked with beta brainwaves and the left hemisphere of the brain – in other words, *stress city*.

When you are looking at the world (literally) with peripheral vision, you immediately enter alpha brainwaves and the right hemisphere of the brain. This is much more relaxing and allows

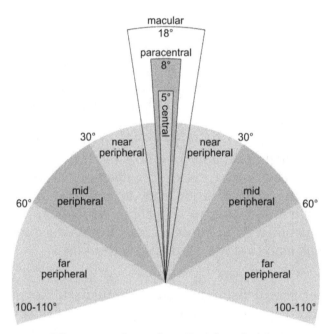

Figure 41: *Central vs. Peripheral vision*
"Peripheral vision" by Zyxwv99 - Own work.
Licensed under CC BY-SA 4.0 via Wikimedia Commons

the subconscious to come into the equation for super learning.

For example, you may recall in chapter 4 we mentioned how the world's greatest speed readers use their peripheral vision to take in entire pages at a time instead of one word at a time.

In his book *Exuberant Animal: The Power of Health, Play and Joyful Movement,* author Frank Forencich says, "We can be sure that long-term overuse of hyperfocused vision, coupled with atrophy of peripheral sensation, will lead to extensive re-wiring of the brain. We can even speculate on a possible link between balanced vision and intelligence. Chronic, tightly focused vision can do amazing things, but it only taps a fraction of our visual-cognitive capability. Monotonous visual inputs may very well lead to static, stereotyped thinking.

"In contrast, a balance of focused and peripheral vision keeps the stimulation moving and taps a far greater percentage of our processing power. Just as chronic overuse of central vision may limit intelligence, active stimulation of our panoramic vision may actually increase it. The message: dumb yourself down with chronic centrally-focused vision; smarten yourself up by relaxing your eyes and letting the periphery in."

Although ophthalmologists seem to agree there's no real way to improve or sharpen peripheral vision, there is scientific research that suggests there are ways to at least improve *peripheral awareness* and the processing of peripheral images.

A few techniques to develop peripheral vision include:

- Widening your vision to something closer to 180 degrees and becoming aware of everything to your extreme left and extreme right.

- Defocus the eyes to counter the hard focus that occurs in central vision.

- Practice eye exercises – especially ones that include a lot of wide-sweeping eye movements.

- Play team sports like soccer or basketball, which force you to constantly use your peripheral vision.

SPEED WRITING

We'd like to offer up one final genius method. However, it's only right to add a disclaimer, pointing out that to our knowledge no studies have been done on it whatsoever. In fact, we are not aware of anyone else ever having mentioned it before – at least not in the way we approach it.

Certainly, there are numerous books and websites devoted to writing manuscripts quickly, but we aren't talking about writers completing entire novels super-fast or students writing essays or letters in half the *normal* time.

Ours is simply an unusual little technique we discovered by accident and noticed it worked wonderfully on many occasions and always when we were severely *time pressured*. We consider this fortuitous discovery an important ingredient in our successes as published authors and feature film screenwriters.

We call it *speed writing*.

This technique, like many of the others listed in this book, no doubt relates to outrunning the conscious mind and going so fast that the superior subconscious is forced to completely take over.

So, as the name suggests, you write so quickly that you don't even know what you're writing anymore. The goal is not to get instantly well-written text, but rather stream-of-consciousness stuff that you can revise and give clearer meaning to later.

According to our experiences, the resulting *stream* will usually have pearls within it, but a lot will need to be edited out as well.

Some of our best plot ideas or character decisions in our novels and film scripts have come using this speed writing technique. We just write super-fast and almost without thinking – maybe for five minutes or so – and more often than not what we wrote solved a major storyline issue or character problem.

It seems that certain insights can only come in this manner – or at least come more easily –

as opposed to writing at regular speed. Sometimes you hit a brick wall when writing novels or screenplays. Something is missing and that something cannot be rectified with the conscious mind no matter how hard you try.

We've also found speed writing is one way to solve the dreaded *writer's block*.

Whether you use this method to add to an existing draft of a document, or whether you're still attempting to complete a first draft, it works. We've proven it to our own satisfaction on numerous occasions.

Speed writing is not just for authors of course. It can be used to good effect by others – students who may be writing essays, for example, or business executives drafting reports or preparing finance proposals. It can even be used in your personal life when you're facing a dilemma and cannot think of any solutions with your conscious mind – in this case you can speed write a list of possible options and see what your subconscious mind delivers to you.

If you want to test the method we use, try the following: put yourself under a time constraint by setting an alarm clock for 5-10 minutes then tell yourself you *must* write as much as you'd normally write in 45-60 minutes. *Go!* Until the alarm clock rings, don't judge yourself or censor yourself or analyze anything – simply write as much as you can, as quickly as you can.

During the process it may feel like you're writing utter garbage, but if our experiences are anything to go by, there will at least be some gems you can retain or use to vastly improve whatever it is you're writing.

Our theory on why speed writing works is that you are not only forcing yourself to operate at speeds that only the subconscious mind can keep up with, but you are also not analyzing, censoring or critiquing what you write as you go (another bad trait of the conscious mind).

The best ideas often seem ridiculous at first and this technique allows you to just get all ideas out of your head and onto paper so you can consider them later.

Exactly how does speed writing relate to genius intelligence? Well, the connection is totally unproven, but instinct and personal experience tells us that, if done correctly (trance-like and without hesitation), you'll tap into that great reservoir of the subconscious mind where all genius abilities come from.

A final point: when speed writing, it's immaterial whether you write with pen in hand or use a computer keyboard. That said, we find speed writing seems to flow better when *handwriting* text – almost as if the pen's a natural extension of the hand, allowing thoughts and words to flow directly from the brain onto the writing pad.

CONNECTING THE DOTS

By now it may be evident that our definition of "genius" differs to yours and, indeed, to the definition held by many. This is not necessarily a sign we are right or wrong. Rather, it's a reflection, perhaps, of the perception the modern world has of genius.

If you don't believe us, ask a hundred people for their definition and you'll likely get a hundred different responses, including widely varying responses.

Though we are not historians, it's our impression that in bygone eras the term *genius* was most used, or, at least often used, when describing brilliant artists like Leonardo da Vinci. Then, in the 20th Century, the term was more often reserved for academics like Albert Einstein. Now, in the 21st Century, it has assumed a broader meaning and is applied to individuals who have achieved extraordinary results in a wide variety of careers, pastimes and fields of endeavor that transcend academia.

Increasingly, we see references in the media and elsewhere to *scientific genius* or *artistic genius* or *sporting genius*, which supports this evolving definition of the word.

Certainly, dictionary definitions (of genius) allow for a broad interpretation. For example, common dictionary definitions include "exceptional intellectual or creative power or other natural ability" and "an exceptionally intelligent person or one with exceptional skill in a particular area of activity."

A cursory look at our Thesaurus offers *mastermind, prodigy, brain, intellect, virtuoso* and even *whiz kid* as alternatives to the word *genius*.

We hope by now it is clear to you that genius can come in many forms besides the obvious academic giants like Einstein and Stephen Hawking – *if* in fact you were ever in doubt.

The term genius can legitimately be applied to certain sportsmen (à la golfer Tiger Woods and tennis player Roger Federer), business executives (Sir Richard Branson and Steve Jobs), artists (Andy Warhol and Jackson Pollock), film directors (Alfred Hitchcock and Stanley Kubrick) – and the list goes on.

For what it's worth, our definition of genius is: *Someone who demonstrates rare intellect, who successfully connects dots between seemingly unconnected things and who sees what others don't to achieve revolutionary outcomes and extraordinary results.*

With that in mind, it may be timely to remind you of what German philosopher Arthur Schopenhauer said about genius: "Talent hits a target no one else can hit. Genius hits a target no one else can see."

Given the examples in this book, it should now be evident there have always been individuals learning at speeds many or most mainstream educationalists would have us believe are not possible.

From speed-reading US presidents like JFK and Roosevelt, to great polymaths such as Archimedes and da Vinci, to savants like Kim Peek and Daniel Tammet, to intelligence agents and their ilk, history is full of people achieving intellectual feats well beyond the norm.

We concede it cannot be proven that elite groups are withholding some of the most advanced learning methods from mainstream society. Even so, it's pretty obvious that little-known accelerated learning techniques do exist in one form or another – techniques (and technologies) capable of increasing IQ.

After reading *Genius Intelligence*, it should also be obvious that geniuses aren't usually born geniuses, or, to put it another way, they *aren't necessarily* born geniuses. Having studied the lives of numerous geniuses, we were surprised to discover most utilized – or, from a young age, were exposed to – various brain activation methods on their respective journeys to becoming acknowledged masters of their fields.

We have detailed, or at least touched on, many of those methods in this book and also given examples of individuals who reached the top of their respective fields employing their favored brain activation methods and disciplines.

We refer to the likes of business tycoons such as Rupert Murdoch who practice Transcendental Meditation, Hollywood stars like Gwyneth Paltrow who consume Ormus and Robin Williams who used isolation tanks. And other examples like bestselling author and life coach Anthony Robbins who mastered speed-reading, Apple founder Steve Jobs who practiced Yoga for mental inspiration, and former world heavyweight boxing champ Mike Tyson who used hypnosis before each fight.

It should now be abundantly clear many of those who reach the top of their fields use rare or little known methods to improve their mental powers to get the jump on the competition – be that in the intelligence, business, political, arts/entertainment, literary or sporting arenas, or, indeed, in any or all sectors of life.

We trust you'll now agree the brain's potential *is* the human potential!

As technology evolves and new scientific breakthroughs occur – such as revolutionary smart drugs and brain stimulation devices – one thing seems certain: super-intelligence will be an option for everyone in the future.

The signs are that future is not far off. For the elite, or for those in the know at least, it seems the future has already arrived . . .

James Morcan & Lance Morcan

If you liked this book, the authors would greatly appreciate a review from you on Amazon.

And if you wish to discuss the material in this book, or other interrelated alternative topics, we invite you to join our Underground Knowledge discussion group on Goodreads: www.goodreads.com

OTHER BOOKS PUBLISHED BY STERLING GATE BOOKS ...

THE UNDERGROUND KNOWLEDGE SERIES

All other books in *The Underground Knowledge Series* are published by Sterling Gate Books. These short, but info-packed non-fiction books are on a vast array of controversial subjects. Each title contains hard-to-find knowledge. *Discover what has been hidden from you . . .*

Garnering evidence from court cases, declassified government files and mainstream media reports, *The Underground Knowledge Series* discloses little-known facts on a wide range of topics. Controversial subjects such as mind control, eugenics, false flag operations, The Queen's hidden assets, secret prisons, The Catcher in the Rye enigma, political assassinations, medical cover-ups, genius intelligence, Yamashita's Gold, the Jonestown mystery, Americanized Nazis, the bankrupting of Third World nations, underground bases, the US Federal Reserve, the New World Order, forbidden science, the War on Drugs, subliminal messages and even extraterrestrials.

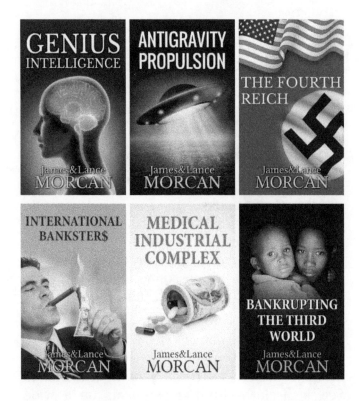

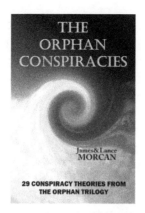

THE ORPHAN CONSPIRACIES:

29 CONSPIRACY THEORIES FROM THE ORPHAN TRILOGY

The Orphan Conspiracies: 29 Conspiracy Theories from The Orphan Trilogy, written by novelists and filmmakers James Morcan & Lance Morcan with a foreword by leading Japanese scientist Dr. Takaaki Musha, contains hard-to-find knowledge. This non-fiction book is based on the political, scientific and financial insights in the Morcans' bestselling international thriller series **The Orphan Trilogy** (novels that merge fact with fiction by incorporating real-world theories on public figures and major organizations). Now the authors provide detailed analysis for each one of those controversial theories.

In many ways, this exhaustively-researched work is the secret history of the 20th and 21st

Centuries. But more than a history, it reveals what is happening **right now** behind the scenes - in underground bunkers, in the corridors of power, in prime banks and meetings of the world's elite.

The Morcans connect the dots between many nefarious events in recent times and strip away the seemingly infinite classified layers of governments and intelligence agencies. Shockingly, they expose a **splinter civilization** operating in our midst that has at its disposal extraordinary suppressed technologies, unlimited resources and enormous black budgets - all inadvertently financed by everyday taxpayers.

Garnering evidence from court cases, declassified government files and mainstream media reports, the authors disclose little-known facts on a wide range of topics. Diverse subjects such as mind control, eugenics, false flag operations, The Queen's hidden assets, secret prisons, The Catcher in the Rye enigma, political assassinations, medical cover-ups, genius learning techniques, Yamashita's Gold, the Jonestown mystery, Americanized Nazis, the bankrupting of Third World nations, underground bases, the US Federal Reserve, the New World Order, forbidden science, the War on Drugs, subliminal messages and even extraterrestrials.

The criminals caught like deer in the headlights of these whistleblowing revelations include corrupt officials, racists, secret society members, warmongers, compromised journalists, economic hitmen, modern-day Doctor Frankensteins and mysterious individuals rumored to have wealth that would dwarf the net worth of Bill Gates and others on Forbes' so-called Rich Lists.

Written from multiple perspectives; at times giving voice to conspiracy theorists; on other occasions siding with sceptics; vacillating between serious investigative writing and tongue-in-cheek, self-deprecating humor - **The Orphan Conspiracies** delivers a balanced exposé of some of the most important issues of our time.

In their unflinching quest for truth and justice, the Morcans take no prisoners as they 'subpoena' the global elite - be they banksters, US Presidents, British Royals, Big Pharma, the Vatican, the FBI, the CIA, the Military Industrial Complex or the founders and CEO's of multinational corporations like Facebook, Google, BP, Microsoft, Shell and Amazon. No suspicious individual or organization is granted immunity in this no-holds-barred trial conducted on behalf of **The People**.

Go beyond rumors and conspiracy theories to documented facts and confirmed reality and **find out just how deep the rabbit hole goes** . . .

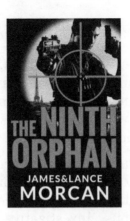

THE NINTH ORPHAN (THE ORPHAN TRILOGY, #1)

An orphan grows up to become an assassin for a highly secretive organization. When he tries to break free and live a normal life, he is hunted by his mentor and father figure, and by a female orphan he spent his childhood with. On the run, the mysterious man's life becomes entwined with his beautiful French-African hostage and a shocking past riddled with the darkest of conspiracies is revealed.

★★★★★ "What makes The Ninth Orphan stand out from other thrillers is its intelligent handling of its themes. Like Kazuo Ishiguro's haunting novel, Never Let Me Go, The Ninth Orphan taps into our fascination with the possibilities of genetic selection, and the consequences it may bring. Throw in a pinch of romance and the suggestion of political shadow organizations that may or may not operate in the real world, and you have an exhilarating read that will keep the little grey cells ticking over long after you've reached the final page."

~ The Flaneur Book Reviews UK

★★★★★ "This psychological thriller really kept me on the edge of my seat!"

~ Susan M. Heim, bestselling author of the 'Chicken Soup for the Soul' series

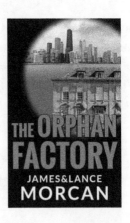

THE ORPHAN FACTORY
(THE ORPHAN TRILOGY, #2)

An epic, atmospheric story that begins with twenty three genetically superior orphans being groomed to become elite spies in Chicago's Pedemont Orphanage and concludes with a political assassination deep in the Amazon jungle.

THE ORPHAN UPRISING
(THE ORPHAN TRILOGY, #3)

In this explosive conclusion to The Orphan Trilogy, the ninth-born orphan's dramatic story resumes five years after book one, The Ninth Orphan, ends.

THE ORPHAN TRILOGY

(THE NINTH ORPHAN / THE ORPHAN FACTORY / THE ORPHAN UPRISING)

Twenty-three orphans with numbers for names from 1 to 23.

Number Nine wants to escape from 'the orphanage.'

Read the highly-rated international conspiracy thriller series in full and at a discounted price. Three novels spanning over 1,000 explosive pages . . .

Book One: THE NINTH ORPHAN

Book Two: THE ORPHAN FACTORY

Book Three: THE ORPHAN UPRISING

Meet Number Nine - an orphan, a spy, a lover . . . a master of disguise, an assassin, a shapeshifter . . . a freedom fighter, a human chameleon, a reformed contract killer.

He's all of the above. He's none of the above.

Nine is enslaved by the Omega Agency, a shadowy organization seeking to create a New World Order. When he tries to break free and live a normal life, Nine is hunted by his mentor and father figure, and by a female orphan he spent his childhood with. On the run, his life becomes entwined with his beautiful French-African hostage and a shocking past is revealed . . . A past that involves the mysterious Pedemont Orphanage in Chicago, Illinois.

Standing in the way of Nine's freedom are his fellow orphans - all elite operatives like himself - who are under orders to terminate him. Nine finds himself in a seemingly infinite maze of cloak and dagger deception. Time and again, he must call on all his advanced training to survive.

But can the ninth-born orphan ever get off the grid? To find out you'll need to go on a tumultuous journey around the world to such far-flung locations as the Arctic, Asia, Europe, the Amazon, Africa and South Pacific islands. **The frenetic cat-and-mouse chase moves from airports to train stations and hidden torture prisons, taking the reader on a page turning, frightening non-stop action ride into the world of corrupted**

power that goes beyond conspiracy theories to painful reality.

Fast-paced, totally fresh and original, filled with deep and complex characters, The Orphan Trilogy is a controversial, high-octane thriller series with an edge. Merging fact with fiction, it illuminates shadow organizations rumored to actually exist in our world. **The three novels explore a plethora of conspiracies involving real organizations like the CIA, MI6, and the UN, and public figures such as President Obama, Queen Elizabeth II as well as the Clinton, Marcos and Bush families.**

The Orphan Trilogy exposes a global agenda designed to keep the power in the hands of a select few. Nine's oppressors are a shadow government acting above and beyond the likes of the White House, the FBI, the Pentagon and the NSA.

One of the Omega Agency's black ops employs MK-Ultra mind control technology on genetically engineered agents to facilitate the agendas of those in power. When Nine successfully deprograms himself from MK-Ultra, all hell breaks loose. But to gain his freedom he must bust out of the Pedemont Orphanage and break into Omega's other orphanages and underground medical laboratories around the world. In the process he uncovers chilling scientific experiments taking place on children. **Could something like this**

ever take place? Or, is it already taking place somewhere in the world right now?

The trilogy also has a poignant, romantic sub-plot. It contains the kind of intimate character portraits usually associated with psychological thrillers.

Book/Film/TV references: The Manchurian Candidate, The Saint, The Da Vinci Code, Bond, Dark Angel, The Jackal, Mission Impossible, Salt, The Pretender, Bourne, The Island, Taken.

This unique, unpredictable and epic spy thriller series covers everything from political assassinations and suppressed science to young adult romance and accelerated learning techniques.

Buckle up for a nail-biter to the very end.

Written by father-and-son writing team Lance & James Morcan (authors of Fiji: A Novel), The Orphan Trilogy was first published in 2013 by Sterling Gate Books. A feature film adaptation of The Ninth Orphan is currently being developed.

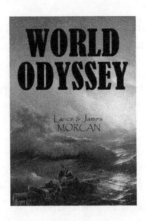

WORLD ODYSSEY
(THE WORLD DUOLOGY, #1)

Set in the nineteenth century, World Odyssey follows the fortunes of three young travelers as each embarks on an epic journey. Their dramatic adventures span sixteen years and see them engage with American Indians, Barbary Coast pirates, Aborigines, Maoris and Pacific Islanders as they travel around the world - from America to Africa, from England to the Canary Islands, to Australia, New Zealand and Samoa.

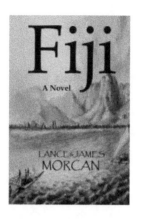

FIJI: A NOVEL
(THE WORLD DUOLOGY, #2)

Fiji is a spellbinding novel of adventure, cultural misunderstandings, religious conflict and sexual tension set in one of the most exotic and isolated places on earth.

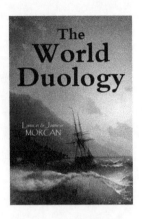

THE WORLD DUOLOGY
(WORLD ODYSSEY / FIJI: A
NOVEL)

Set in the nineteenth century, The World Duology (World Odyssey / Fiji: A Novel) follows the fortunes of three young travelers. Their dramatic adventures span sixteen years and see them engage with American Indians, Barbary Coast pirates, Aborigines, Maoris and Pacific Islanders as they travel around the world - from America to Africa, from England to the Canary Islands, to Australia, New Zealand, Samoa and Fiji.

In book one, World Odyssey, ambitious American adventurer Nathan Johnson, sheltered English missionary Susannah Drake and irrepressible Cockney Jack Halliday each follow very different paths.

Nathan's journey begins when runs away to sea and finds himself the slave of a Northwest American Indian tribe after his ship founders on the rocky coast; Susannah's journey begins after she agrees to accompany her clergyman father to Fiji to help him run a mission station there, and they must endure a nightmare voyage they're lucky to survive; Jack's journey begins when he's sentenced to seven years' hard labor in the British penal colony of New South Wales after stealing hemp from an unscrupulous employer.

After traveling thousands of miles and experiencing the best and worst that life can offer, these three disparate individuals eventually end up in the remote archipelago of Fiji, in the South Pacific, where their lives intersect.

In book two, Fiji: A Novel, Jack sets himself up to trade Fijian kauri to European traders while Nathan trades muskets to the same natives Susannah and her father are trying to convert to Christianity. Conflict's inevitable.

Susannah despises Nathan, but is also attracted to him. She soon finds she's torn between her spiritual and sexual selves.

When their lives are suddenly endangered by marauding cannibals, all three are forced to rely on each other for their very survival.

Written by father-and-son writing team Lance & James Morcan (authors of The Orphan Trilogy), The World Duology is an epic historical adventure series published by Sterling Gate Books. A feature film adaptation of Fiji is currently being developed.

★★★★★ "I was immediately drawn into the story, and the fast-paced action kept me turning the pages until the end. The historical and cultural details made it a highly interesting book offering an insight into the anthropological issues at a time when conflicts between different ethnic groups were solved by brutal violence. Between romance, action and historical accuracy, this story has all the elements of great entertainment. I would highly recommend this book to readers who enjoy historical fiction or epic adventures."

~ Karine Brégeon (author of 'Francette and the Mystery of the Deaf Soldier')

★★★★★ "Great adventure"

~ Lynelle Clark (author of 'A Pirate's Wife')

★★★★★ "Historic fiction at its best"

~ J.B. DiNizo (author of 'Comings and Goings')

★★★★★ "A truly gripping epic James Michener style!"

~ Historical Novel Review